WHERE WILL

Where Will I Find the Time?

SALLY McCLUNG

YOUTH WITH A MISSION
AMSTERDAM

KINGSWAY PUBLICATIONS
EASTBOURNE

Cover design by Drummond Chapman

British Library Cataloguing in Publication Data

McClung, Sally
    Where will I find the time?
    1. Christian life. Time. Allocation
    I. Title
    248.4

    ISBN 0-86065-539-3

Youth With A Mission (YWAM) is an international movement of
Christians from many denominations, united in Christ and
dedicated to presenting him personally to this generation.
Youth With A Mission, 50 Prins Hendrikkade,
1012 AC Amsterdam, Holland

Printed in Great Britain for
KINGSWAY PUBLICATIONS LTD
Lottbridge Drove, Eastbourne, E. Sussex BN23 6NT by
Richard Clay Ltd, Bungay, Suffolk.
Typeset by CST, Eastbourne, E. Sussex.

This book is thankfully dedicated to my husband, Floyd, who during the years of our life together has patiently walked with me through the various learning stages of how to use my time effectively for the Lord.

Contents

	Introduction	10
1.	A Time to Organize	12
2.	A Time to Build	28
3.	A Time for Marriage	38
4.	A Time for Family	50
5.	A Time for Friendship	66
6.	A Time for Life	80
7.	A Time for Work	91
8.	A Time for Fun	103
9.	A Time for Healing	112
	A Last Word	123
	Further Reading	125

Take Time

Take time to think—it is the source of power.
Take time to play—it is the secret of perpetual
  youth.
Take time to read—it is the fountain of wisdom.
Take time to pray—it is the greatest power on
  earth.
Take time to love and be loved—it is a God-given
  privilege.
Take time to be friendly—it is the road to
  happiness.
Take time to laugh—it is the music of the soul.

Take time to give—it is too short a day to be
  selfish.
Take time to work—it is the price of success.

Introduction

Time is one of the world's deepest mysteries. No one can say exactly what it is. Yet the ability to measure it makes our way of life possible; the ability to use it properly makes our life fulfilling—or frustrating. Time is a very specific gift that God has given to us. For many, it's a gift that is still in its package—unknown, unused, unappreciated. We haven't unwrapped it and learned how to take care of it. Time is a unique gift, but one that can't be developed until we've read the instructions and applied them.

Ecclesiastes 3:1 says, 'There is a time for everything, and a season for every activity under heaven.' God has given us time for all the dimensions of our lives, but all too often we haven't learned how to use that time properly.

> I have only just a minute,
> only 60 seconds in it.
>
> Forced upon me—can't refuse it,
> but it is up to me to use it.
>
> I must suffer if I lose it,
> give account if I abuse it.

> Just a tiny little minute,
>   but eternity is in it.

Someone has said that 'man's idea of eternity may be known by the use he makes of time.' This book is about the use of our time—taking time for all the God-given dimensions of life. The principles are simple and basic ones, enabling us to control our lives (and not be controlled) and to find time for everything.

I

A Time to Organize

'A time to search and a time to give up, a time to keep and a time to throw away' (Ecclesiastes 3:6).

My mother once told me that I must have been born with a computer in my brain! Ever since I was a little girl, I'd always tidied drawers and cupboards, and helped her get our household organized. Although organization is something that comes very naturally to me, I have found over the years that I have still had a lot to learn. It is a gift that God has put within me, but I have had to learn to develop it according to his ways and standards.

All of us relate to time in different ways: referees call time, prisoners serve time, musicians mark time, historians record time, loafers kill time, and statisticians keep time. No matter how we relate to time, the fact is that all of us are given the same amount. Time is the great equalizer! There are only 24 hours in a day and 168 hours in a week. God wants us to use them in a way that extends and builds up his kingdom. We need to learn how to manage our time because it is the only way we will get the time, the opportunity to think, and the freedom to do the jobs that God has put before us—the ones he is calling us to. God wants to teach us in this area. The goal of time management is to analyse, to manage and to consolidate. Many time-management principles are basic, but how we apply them is very varied and personal. Schedules, systems and formats have to be adapted and altered to fit our own individual situations. We don't have to get locked into someone else's programme just because an expert says it works.

I have often heard it said that if you want to get something done, ask a busy person to do it. That sounds rather contradictory, yet it is true. The reason is that a busy person has learned how to use his time effectively. Busy people seem to have the most time because they leave so little to circumstance. They plan. They can always manage to do more because they know how to put it together properly. When we are organized we run our life on schedule, otherwise it will run us! The choice is ours. Scheduling our time gives us freedom to do what God has given us to do. Ecclesiastes 8:5 says, 'The wise heart will know the proper time and procedure.' There is much that God wants to teach us in wisdom and time management.

Besides being a wife and mother, my schedule involves a lot of other responsibilities. I am a member of the local leadership team for the missionary organization that my husband, Floyd, and I are part of. I speak regularly at women's seminars and leadership gatherings. I am involved in a number of regular counselling situations, and also correspond with many woman leaders in our organization in various parts of the world. I am involved in several annual training programmes that we sponsor, and I am part of the hospitality ministry for our work in Amsterdam. We also have many guests in our home. Needless to say. I've had to learn how to organize my time. There are a number of specific areas we need to give attention to in learning to control our time.

A time budget

Time is precious. It can't be stored or saved. It must be used properly. We need to learn to budget our time. We usually think of budgeting in terms of finance. I believe God wants to teach us to budget our time as well as our money. In fact, we need to budget our time as carefully as thrifty people budget money. We need to learn how to do things on a fixed income of 24 hours a day—to purchase the necessities and luxuries of life on that income. That's all we have to work with. We often overestimate what we can do in one day, and underestimate what we can do in a week. God wants to bring us into balance here. In learning to budget our time, we need to make a list of our activities and the time we spend on them.

Athletes know: the more you do, the more you can do. Most of us are aware that the less we do, the more tired, dissatisfied, and frustrated we become. We need to make our 24-hour time budget work effectively for us—not just coping but creating, and using our time to greater advantage. Nothing fuels those creative fires like success, including the success of seeing our time budget working. How we use our 24-hour budget will determine our success or failure in every area of our life.

We should think of our day in terms of three segments: morning, afternoon and evening. This gives us 21 segments during the week. We can often accomplish more if we think of the work before us in terms of those segments. If we break it down into hour or half-hour parts, we may get exasperated because many of the things we want to do can't be accomplished within these small time frames. However, they can be accomplished in a couple of mornings or afternoons. We can then learn to plan our week's activities in terms of these 21 segments.

Setting goals

In order to establish our goals, we must begin by listing the tasks we need to accomplish in the areas of responsibility God has given us. Ephesians 5:16 encourages us to make the most of the time we have. We need to set deadlines—time frameworks for goals that God has given us. I once read an article that said that the words 'as soon as possible', when referring to time, are actually quite meaningless. Does, 'as soon as possible' mean tomorrow, next week or next month? We need to train ourselves to be much more specific. It is better to set a time framework and be off than not to set a time framework at all—we can always readjust when we see that we have aimed incorrectly. A time framework gives us something specific to work with. Without such specification we often just flounder and waste time. Set goals and be specific about how long they'll take to be achieved.

In talking about goals, we need to look at four areas that relate to our lives and ministry in accomplishing what God has for us. First of all, we need to think in terms of *long-term projects* that we are working on. These may be personal projects, or ones related to our job. They may be creative projects, or plans for our home or family. In each of these areas I have set goals prayerfully with the Lord's help. They are long-term goals, but I am working towards them. The most common mistake we as Christians make is not planning for the future. We plan for next week or maybe six months from now, but we don't look far enough down the line to set those long-term goals. Many challenges will never be accomplished if we do not think long-range.

Secondly, we must look at the *monthly* goals that God has for us. My husband, Floyd, and I have found this very helpful to do together. I count it a wonderful privilege to be able to work with my husband in what God has called us to do. It is a great joy for me to work together with my partner in Christian service. However, this is not something that just happens—it is something that Floyd and I have to work at. We have to plan. We used to do this weekly. Now we do it monthly—or sometimes even several months in advance. We sit down and co-ordinate our activity and ministry together. Christian couples can tend to grow in different directions in the midst of the busyness of working for the Lord. We're often so involved in our individual activities that we're going in opposite directions, doing totally different things from our partner. Our lives can become so separate that there is little 'meshing', and we can easily become independent and self-sufficient.

We have found it very helpful not only to have personal monthly goals, but also to have monthly goals for things we're going to do together as a couple. There are often people with whom we want to build relationships and friendships. There may be other Christian leaders that we want to meet with in the country where we live or in other countries. Perhaps there are people that we want to spend time with in counselling. There are usually activities that we want to do as a couple or as a family. We plan these things into our goals and into our schedule. It also helps us to know what the other is doing. When we sit down and co-ordinate our month together, I feel a part of Floyd's life even when he is off doing something else, and vice versa. We can then commit these goals to the Lord and work together as a team, even though we're working separately.

Breaking it down a little further, we need to look at our *weekly* goals. Plan ahead for the week. I find it helpful to sit down on Saturday or Sunday for 15 to 30 minutes, look at the schedule for the coming week, and begin to plan ahead for it. Are there special things that I must do? Do I need to get materials together for some project I'm working on? Do I need to get up earlier some days and plan that into my schedule with my family? Do I need more rest because certain activities are going to take a lot out of me? I can look at my week's goals and learn how to manage my time in order to see these goals accomplished effectively.

Then, of course, there are our *daily* goals. We should work from the long-range down to the monthly, the weekly and then the daily. Our long-term goals will only become manageable if we break them down within smaller time frameworks. If we have a long-range goal for something we want to see accomplished a year from now, we should begin to think what steps we need to take each week and each day in order to see it accomplished. Psalm 90:12 urges, 'So teach us to number our days, that we may apply our hearts unto wisdom' (Authorised Version). God wants to show us how to organize our day and set the appropriate goals.

As God puts specific goals on our hearts, then, we must look at them and break them down so that they are manageable and achievable. We mustn't allow our emotions to guide our activities. We may not always feel like finishing a job, but we can discipline ourselves to achieve our goals whether we feel like it or not. When there is too much to do, there's often a tendency to worry and agonize over it. Someone once said, 'Worry is like a rocking-chair. It gives you something to do but it doesn't get you anywhere.' As we look at all the things we want to do, and decide where to go with our goal-planning, I suggest that we need to set priorities.

Setting priorities

We must ask the Lord for his help in setting priorities for the goals we now have before us. We need *his* sense of priority. Remember, Christ left some things undone. We can't do it all. Proverbs 16:3 says, 'Commit thy works unto the Lord, and thy thoughts shall be established' (Authorised Version). We must ask the Lord to establish our thoughts in understanding priorities. We must wait for his orders and then receive his strength to carry them out. Many times (most!) I find that God's order is very different from Sally's. I carefully pray through the goals the Lord has for me, and assume that the order to go about them is 1, 2, 3. But the Lord may be thinking 2, 1, 3. I need prayerfully to look at the things before me and make priorities with the Lord's help. Because I am naturally organized, this is very important for me. I could rely on my own skills, my own ability to plan, but God wants to guide me and help me. He wants to use the gift he's placed in me. I don't just ignore that gift, but allow God to bring about a balanced attitude to it in developing it responsibly and depending on him.

As I establish priorities, I make a list of what needs to be done in each of the four goal areas: long range, monthly, weekly and daily. For each area I list what is most important, next important, and work my way down. Making priorities is evaluating what is really important. Once we've done that, then we can organize and plan ahead. I continue to ask the Lord if there are any areas that I should cut out. Am I trying to do too much? Are there things that will distract me from the main purpose God has for my life? I also ask the Lord if there are any areas that are to be combined. Sometimes goals can be combined for greater effectiveness.

It's good to keep a time log for a period—maybe a week or a month. Write down everything that is done and how much time is spent doing it. Then sit down and evaluate. This is often done in the business world, but I think we would benefit from it in our personal lives. Effective executives find out where their time is actually going. They look at it very specifically. We could be more effective in our time management if we would do that as well. Although we are 'led by the Spirit', human responsibility enters in as well.

It is important in establishing priorities to plan in all of our activities. If I'm struggling in having a regular quiet time, I need to plan that into my day so that it doesn't get squeezed out in the busyness of the day. Every day in my agenda I have 'quiet time' written at the top of the list—it is a protection to me so that this very crucial part of my life with the Lord doesn't get eliminated in all that I'm doing for him. If the Lord is speaking to me about my health and I need to exercise regularly, I put that into my schedule. All activities—large and small—go into the schedule, then I sort them into priorities.

I was struck once when reading about the life of Jacqueline Kennedy Onassis. A very well-known woman, she has at times carried a lot of responsibility in her life. She keeps an hourly schedule! Not just a monthly, weekly or daily schedule—but an hourly one. I was very very challenged by that. If this woman, who has done many wonderful things in the world at various times in her life (albeit things that aren't perhaps counting for eternity), sees it as being important to keep an hourly schedule, how much more do I as a Christian woman need to accept my responsibility seriously in the use of my time.

We must work our priorities into our time budget. We have to be realistic, remembering again that the budget is only 24 hours a day. We identify and eliminate the things that don't need to be done in working up the budget. Then we remind ourselves of Ecclesiastes 3:1—'There is a time for everything, and a season for every activity under heaven.' Now we're ready to move forward with the Lord's help to see these things accomplished.

Once we've made priorities, we must do our best to stick to that timetable. We have to make priorities and then be careful *not to make apologies*. If God has given us a sense of priority, we need to work within that and not go around apologizing all the time for things we can't do. That's hard, I know. It's especially difficult when faced with the needs of people all around us. We want to help them, minister to them—yet we are not God, and we can't do everything or please everyone. I'll say more later about flexibility. The point here is to establish our priorities and stick to them with the fear of the Lord upon us because he has helped us to establish them.

A personal agenda

A friend of mine was asking about this book when I was still in the process of writing. When I told him it was on the use of time, he said, 'I hope you're not just going to tell me I should use an agenda.' Well, that's not all I have to say, but a personal agenda is certainly a vital tool.

An important part of time management is the agenda that is used to co-ordinate one's activities. An agenda is simply a fancy name for a book where you can make lists of all the things you need to do. I make a note of appointments with people, meetings I need to attend, speaking engagements, my children's school activities, household jobs, projects I'm working on, birthdays—anything and everything. My agenda helps me to co-ordinate all my activities as smoothly as possible. I also have a place in my agenda for other information that I want to keep handy—the numbers of my credit card, driver's licence and passport; addresses and phone numbers; ideas for presents for my family; a list of books I want to read; projects I want to do when I have time. My agenda is a vital tool in helping me to organize my life.

There are many different types of agendas—all in various shapes, sizes and forms. Just find the one that works for you. Many people in the organization that I'm part of use the Youth With A Mission Renewal Diary put out by our base in Tyler, Texas. It's been a real God-send for them. A number of the men in leadership use the Time Manager. I walked all over the city of Amsterdam one day looking for an agenda that would fit my schedule and my lifestyle. I finally found one that was fairly suitable and could be adapted to the things I wanted. Whatever kind it is, find one that meets your needs. Don't think you've got to use one kind just because everybody else is using it. It may be different, but find one that works for you.

Once you've found the one for you—use it! Use it to organize your daily goals. Pray over it each day. I find this helpful to do the night before. Just before I go to bed, I sit down and look at the next day's schedule. I pray over the activities I have felt led to participate in and be part of. I commit the next day to the Lord. It brings a sense of rest and peace in my heart as I am getting ready for bed. I am not going to bed worrying about all the activities of the next day. I have given it to the Lord. I am trusting him to help me with it step by step. This can be done in the morning just as well, of course. However, I find that as a mother my days always get off to a busy start. When I get out of bed in the morning there are many demands upon my time in getting my children off to school, helping Floyd get co-ordinated for the day, cooking breakfast, and getting dressed and ready for my day. Morning is usually a very hectic time for me, so it's better to pray over my day the night before. Whatever time works best—the important thing is to pray over the day.

I find it helpful to write things down in sequence for the day in my agenda. I go through the list and number things by priority. That way I can look at my day's schedule at a glance and see what needs my attention first, secondly and so on. It helps me keep control over my day, so my time doesn't get wasted as I move from one thing to the next. When I finish one thing, I know immediately what to go to next. Don't overschedule—it always causes problems. We must allow time here and there for the unforeseen, for the unknown, for interruptions and for emergencies.

Always have a master list of what you need to do that you can refer to. I think this is important in all four goal areas, especially the daily area. Don't try to keep everything in your head and remember it—it will be frustrating and tiring, and you will find that you forget a lot. When you write things down, it is the very first step towards seeing them accomplished. You may find it helpful to cross things off your list when you get them done. Floyd teases me about doing that. As I go through my day, I cross things off as I complete them. Once I have a full day done, I put a great big slash across the page to show that that day is finished. I've done my best with it. I look at that little page and I feel as if I have accomplished something. It brings a personal sense of satisfaction to me. It is one of those little idiosyncrasies that we all have. I thought I was really weird until I read in a time manager journal of someone else (who is very well known and respected) who does this too. I decided that I can't be too weird after all.

Evaluate your day at the end of it and learn from it. I think this is something we can never get away from. Time management and time use does improve with practice and working at it. If you are struggling in this area, remember there is hope. If you are just learning, there is a lot of room to grow. It does improve as you learn from what you've done and work at it.

Checklists

'The faintest scrawl is mightier than the strongest memory.' I like that! Because I am a very organized, detailed person, I am always thinking of things. I can be in the middle of a fabulous time of worship and have a thought flash through my mind about something totally unrelated. I quickly get out my little pad and pen and write it down. Then I don't have to worry about remembering it. I get teased about this quite regularly. Sometimes people come up to me later and ask what I was writing down. This system is freeing to me. Because I've got it down, I'm not going to forget it. Many times I've seen that the thought is an inspiration from the Lord. When I quickly jot it down on paper, it doesn't distract me from what I am doing at the present. I am free to give myself fully to the situation at hand . . . but I do not forget what has come to my mind. The business world understands the importance of this. It's called the W.E.D. principle—write everything down!

Be prepared! Always have something with you for making a quick list. I have a small note-pad (it fits into a normal sized pocket) which I carry with me wherever I go. With it is a pen, a small plastic calendar for the current year that also has measurements along the edges, a few paper clips, and several 'post it' stickers. It's like a miniature office. I use it everywhere.

When we make a checklist it's important that we look at it. I have some friends that are great at making lists, then they tuck them away somewhere and never use them. A checklist is your best friend—it saves you time, steps and energy. A checklist is meant to be a tool, so put it somewhere where you will see it regularly. If that is in your agenda, put it there alongside your daily schedule. If it is in your Bible, put it there. If it is in the middle of your bathroom mirror, then stick it up there. Put it where it will be a help and tool to you.

Set up a system for jogging your memory. There are a lot of different systems for this. I use my agenda, right next to my Bible. These two things are with me almost all the time. I mark everything down in my agenda. Maybe you have another system. Whatever is most effective for you, set up your own system for jogging your memory and remembering the things you put on your checklist.

Keep a calendar in a prominent place to remind you of dates that are coming up. Even if you function well with an agenda, it doesn't hurt to have something else in another place in your home to remind you of points in your agenda. Maybe you will want one in your office and one in your home, as well as using your agenda. A small notice-board is also very helpful. You can put up little notes and reminders. Take advantage of tools like this to help you make the best use of your time.

A checklist is meant to be a helpful tool. If we overdo it, of course, it becomes a time waster. We don't want to spend all our time making lists instead of doing what's on them!

The starting point

You may not be an organized person naturally. You may be thinking this all sounds impossible. You may say, 'That's OK for Sally. She woke up when she was born and was able to start organizing those drawers for her mother, but it just isn't me.' Well, OK. But you can change; you can learn; you can grow. It can become a mark of your lifestyle that you manage time well. One can never catch up with good intentions—'It is better to look ahead and prepare than to look back and regret.' I believe there are two motivations that bring a person to that point of change.

The first is discontent with where you are. You may look at your life and realize that you are frustrated that your time isn't being used well. You're not getting the things done that God has put on your heart. Consequently, discontent is growing inside you. Don't ignore that. I believe God has put it there because he is trying to speak to you about growth in this area.

The second motivation for change is prayer—seeking God for how he would like things to be. I find it important to do this regularly. I make changes in my schedule all the time. I don't just seek the Lord, ascertain what I think is right, and then leave it like that for the next year. I am constantly lifting up to him the things that I am doing, the things that are in my agenda, in the weekly and daily time budget. I regularly ask the Lord what adjustments I need to make. Our schedule is not a road that we start travelling along, never turning right or left. We need to be prayerfully open to change. Learning how to use our time in this way is a lifestyle God has for us.

Your colleagues, your husband or wife, your children, your neighbours, your room-mate—those that you work and live with—all appreciate order . . . in the home, in the office, and in the work situation. Confusion, chaos and disarray do not bring a sense of peace and well-being to people around us. As we learn how to use our time and bring order to our lives, it helps bring about the right atmosphere for our home and ministry. God is a God of order. We see that in all that he has created. He has also created us to appreciate order and to build it into our lives.

The more you do, the more you can do. I believe God wants to stretch us. He wants to teach us to manage our time. He wants to keep teaching us as we learn and grow so that we can take on greater visions and challenges for him. There is a world that is still not evangelized. God called us to do that, and he wants to stretch us so we can. It starts in our heart in the place of prayer, but it comes into the practical arena in our daily lives in learning how to use our time wisely. Scheduling gives freedom. Many people think it brings bondage, but just the opposite is true. It brings freedom to do the things God has for us.

Nothing lifts morale like the sense of satisfaction in a job well done. God wants to teach us to use our time well so we can accomplish things for him. Remember that your schedule will change as your life changes. Don't become so static that you miss the prompting and the moving of the Holy Spirit. I like something that I heard Floyd say once: 'The purpose of being organized is not to get ahead of the Holy Spirit but just to keep up with him!' The Holy Spirit is on the move in this day and age. He is doing wonderful things. Around the world fires of revival are growing. They have been little sparks, but they are starting to burn into little bushes of fire. Something is happening. God is at work. The Holy Spirit wants us to keep up with what he is doing in our midst. In order to do that effectively and efficiently we have to learn how to use that time budget he has given us. So it is not unspiritual to be practical in learning to use our time well.

Even with the best scheduling and time management, there are occasions when we just don't get everything done—at least, not on time. Interruptions, unexpected things and delays all keep us from achieving our goals. The important thing is not to give up. Don't accept defeat. If you accept it in one area, it's an attitude that quickly spreads to others. Keep plugging away. The old saying 'better late than never' certainly applies here. We learn by trial and error. As we keep trying, we will learn and grow in this area.

In the chapters ahead, we'll look at other details of taking time to organize. Topics such as delegating, interruptions, wasting time, learning to refuel, and our individual levels of energy will be considered and their practical application discussed. There are many areas of fine tuning in time management. The important thing is to get a foundation laid on which to build. There is a time to organize. If you've not done it yet, the time is now!

> Yesterday is a cancelled cheque.
> Tomorrow is a promissory note.
> Today is the only cash you have.
> Spend it wisely!

The best way to begin to 'spend' today is to develop our relationship with God.

2

A Time to Build

'A time to scatter stones and a time to gather them'
(Ecclesiastes 3:5).

As Christians there is more to being good managers of
our time than simply learning organizational skills.
Organizing ourselves is not enough—there must be
something underneath. In taking time to build, we
must make sure we establish a foundation—our daily
walk with God. We must take time for God. Each of us
needs to stop every day, turn off the world, and take
time to talk to God . . . and give him time to talk to us.
In the midst of busy schedules, time pressures, and
the stress of daily life, that daily quiet time with God
is usually the first thing to disappear. We can't let that
happen if we expect to lead effective lives as Christians
in the midst of a difficult world. I know all too well that
I can't get along without him, but he can get along
without me. God will survive, although he longs for
that fellowship with us, but we will suffer and find
ourselves lacking because of not having spent time in
his presence.

Our devotional life must never be casual. A regular
devotional time may be difficult, but it is not impos-

sible. It must be worked into our time budget and placed at the top of the list as a priority. A quiet time during the course of our day is what gives our spiritual life depth. Our devotional life keeps us centred on to-day, where God wants it to be—in the present rather than in the past or future. When we realize our deep need for time with God it is easy to put it in the place of priority in our daily schedule that it needs to be. Some-one once said, 'Backsliding begins when knee-bend-ing stops.' We must make our quiet time the number one item on our daily agenda in terms of priority. 'A quiet time with God is worth a lifetime with man.'

Perhaps it's helpful to remind ourselves of why it is so important to spend time in the word and in the presence of our Father. The following points were made by Joy Dawson at a lecture I attended.

▷ Without it we will cease to see things from his divine perspective. Only when we see what God says can we have God's view (Psalm 119:102).

▷ Without it, we will have a distorted view of truth (Psalm 119:30).

▷ Unless we have God's help and direction, we will make wrong choices in our life (Psalm 19:7, 8, 11; 119:1, 104, 105).

▷ We will live in confusion and frustration without spending time understanding his word (Psalm 119: 44, 45, 130).

▷ We cannot grow and become spiritually mature without regular spiritual food (Luke 8:12–15).

▷ We cease to have spiritual perception unless we are spending time seeing the world from God's view-point (Psalm 119:98–100; Jeremiah 6:10, 19).

We have an inner vacuum that is waiting to be filled with the presence of the Lord through spending time with him. The human spirit becomes a 'junk receptacle' filled with whatever is nearest unless we are making sure it is filled properly. We are designed to be filled with the power and presence of God. Too often we are haphazardly filled with the trivia of the world. We must take time to meet with him and be filled with his life and Spirit.

When to meet

Time with God should not be a chore. Our devotional life gives meaning to everything we do. One pastor's wife said, 'It is easy to fall into the trap of believing that having a quiet time is just another meaningless habit. But much of life is habit—eating and sleeping, for example. So what difference does it make if your quiet time is a habit? It's a very good habit.' Our quiet time is certainly a habit that we need to establish, but we must be very careful not to let it become mere form lacking in life. It should be an exciting part of our daily schedule.

We often struggle to find a time and system for our quiet time that works for us and that we are happy with. We must carefully examine our own lifestyle, personality, ways of learning and the daily demands made upon us in order to find the most meaningful agenda for our personal worship and devotional life. Our time with the Lord feeds our spirit when the demands of life are crowding in on us and we feel we can't cope. I'm sure that's why Jesus told us to draw ourselves regularly away from the world. When we do, he gives us whatever we need at that particular point in our lives. Any time of the day that works is fine, but being regular and consistent is the key. Maybe you are the type of person who wants to meet with the Lord as soon as you wake up in the morning. Or perhaps you like to spend time with him just before going to bed (just make sure you're not so tired that you fall asleep). I've found my time with the Lord has changed through the years as the schedule of my family has changed. There's no 'magic formula' or certain time of day that is most holy. God is available twenty-four hours a day.

The struggle for discipline in this area of our lives is a big one. But be encouraged—you're not alone. This same battle rages in every Christian. Romans 7:21–24 points out that this struggle is not new. Many through the ages have endeavoured to be disciplined and consistent in doing what they know to be right. We win only as we achieve a constant walk with the Lord. Discipline is a matter of the inner reign of the Lord Jesus. He (and we) will be victorious when he is allowed full rulership in our lives.

I've talked with so many people who have lived with constant guilt because they've not been able to establish a consistent time with the Lord. I think it is important to remember that the bottom line in our devotional life is that it is a relationship. I have a wonderful friendship and relationship with my husband Floyd. He travels a lot and there are times when days go by and I haven't been able to talk to him. I miss this communication and long for it, but our relationship is still there. The same is true with the Lord. He longs to meet with us and talk to us, but our relationship doesn't disappear if we fail in doing that. He understands the pressures of a new baby, several small toddlers that we have to keep up with, times of illness, extra work and pressure on the job, and periods of giving over and above the call of duty in ministry. He understands and he doesn't hold it against us—as we tend to do to ourselves. But these periods mustn't become permanent. We must continue in our goal to find a daily time we can set aside to be with God.

It says in the Bible that 'Abraham walked with God . . . Noah walked with God . . . Enoch walked with God'. When we walk with someone we can talk to them all the time, even as we're busy with other things. We can talk to the Lord while we're washing dishes, ironing, driving or on the train to work. We often overlook times in our schedule when we can be with the Lord. Time management helps us learn to use all our time well and effectively.

When we walk with someone we can also be silent. In fact, the better we know the person we're walking with the more relaxed we are in their presence. We often just enjoy being with them. We also listen when we walk with them for whatever they might have to say. As we walk with God through our daily lives, we need to be careful not to miss the joy of being with him and the opportunity of hearing him speak to us. We don't have to be down on our knees for him to speak— he loves to converse with us throughout the day.

Where to meet

Just as the particular time of day when we have our quiet time is not holy or unholy, so is the place. We can meet with God anywhere. I love the way this poem expresses that:

A Holy Place

My kitchen table is my trysting place
    For there I meet my Saviour face to face.
I find sweet fellowship with Jesus here,
    And leave with Him my daily load of care.

Here family, one by one, are brought before the
   Lord,
And here I learn, and grow, and feast upon His
   word.
O sacred place and hour . . . aglow with His grace,
My kitchen has become a holy place.

                                    Gladys Seashore

We can walk, sit or kneel when we spend time with
the Lord. The position is not holy. The important thing
is to be meeting regularly with our Father. When Floyd
and I were first married and started having times of
prayer together, we ran into a problem—he's a walker
and I'm a sitter! I couldn't understand how he could
concentrate while he was walking around. He couldn't
see how I stayed awake while I sat quietly. It was a
little difficult for a while but we soon learned to compromise. In fact, because I have learned from Floyd
how to walk and pray, I now use my times of walking
around Amsterdam as wonderful times of prayer.

You may find you establish a regular 'prayer closet'.
That's fine as long as you don't limit your time with
the Lord to that particular place. I have a favourite
chair I like to sit in for my quiet time. But I know the
Lord isn't limited to that place. If I have my quiet time
in a different place, he's there too.

How long to meet

We must not shortchange God in our time with him.
The amount of time spent with God is not the key
issue, but obviously the more we put into our quiet
time the more we will come away with. I heard of one
pastor's wife who burns a candle during her
devotional time. This serves as a visible reminder of
how much time she is spending with the Lord. In

regard to regular time alone with God, the old saying is certainly true: 'All of life [and especially spiritual life] is an echo—giving back exactly what we put into it.'

We don't need great amounts of time when we first begin, but we do need regular times, as has already been stated. We often don't spend *any* time with the Lord because we don't have *lots* of time! Start small if you're struggling with regular quiet times. Become disciplined in small amounts of time and let them grow into larger ones as the pattern becomes established. We often bite off more than we can chew to begin with, get discouraged, and give up.

Whatever the amount of time we're working with, we need to learn how to shut the door on the world, draw apart, and spend time with our Father. The Creator of the universe wants to be with us—what greater appointment could we have? A dear friend of mine put it so well when he said, 'We spend time in the Lord's presence awaiting a call from the one whose orders we have loved to follow.' It is in our devotional time that we receive our orders for the day.

Perhaps one of the greatest hindrances to our times of intimacy with the Lord is hurriedness. Intimacy with our Father cannot be rushed. To meet with God takes time. We live in the day and age of instant everything. However, we cannot build an instant spiritual foundation. A solid, sure foundation in our Christian life takes time. Our hurriedness is often really a cover for not taking the time to make priorities and be disciplined. We're so busy—but busy about what? Is anything really more important than meeting with God? Calvin Miller says in his book *The Table of Inwardness* (InterVarsity Press): 'No one who hurries into the presence of God is content to remain for long. Those who hurry in, hurry out. Holy leisure prepares us to receive the gift of inwardness.'

In our walk with God, he adjusts his pace to ours. He knows we're slowed down with small children, illness, ministry, etc. But he can help us carry those loads as we make the effort to meet regularly with him.

> We mutter and sputter,
>   We fume and we spurt.
> We mumble and grumble,
>   Our feelings get hurt.
> We can't understand things,
>   Our vision grows dim,
> When all that we need is:
>   A moment with *him*!
>
> (author unknown)

How to meet

It is helpful to have your devotional materials readily available. You may have a study desk or a corner table where you can keep them. If you have to search for your materials or collect them from scattered areas, it often puts your quiet time back into the chore area.

Various ingredients are needed for our foundation building. Obviously, the Bible is one. I have found the new *One-Year Bible* to be very helpful for my quiet times. It contains 365 daily readings from the Old Testament, New Testament, Psalms and Proverbs. Pick a version of the Bible that you are comfortable with and that communicates clearly to your everyday life. You may also find that a devotional guide with daily thoughts and practical applications is a blessing.

Prayer is another vital ingredient. It was one of the secrets of Christ's work. In Mark's account of Jesus' busy day he says, 'Very early in the morning, while it was still dark, Jesus got up, left the house and went off to a solitary place where he prayed' (Mark 1:35). Christ spent time in the Father's presence and waited for his instructions for the day. Jesus didn't have a divinely drawn blueprint. He discerned the Lord's will day by day as he spent time in prayer.

Praise is also an important part of our quiet time. Praise is giving to God in worship and adoration. It is thanksgiving for the gift and praise to the giver. Prayer is incomplete without praise—it's like life without breath. Praise is loving God for who he is. I've been married a long time, but I still enjoy hearing my husband tell me that he loves me. God is delighted when we express our love to him in worship—no matter how many times we've done it before. You may enjoy listening to worship tapes as part of your quiet time, or you may want to sing songs of praise on your own to him. As we give in worship to the Lord, he ministers to us in our own spirits. Sometimes we're almost too tired to give to the Lord in this way, but as we make the effort to give to him what he so deserves, we are, paradoxically, strengthened in the process.

It is helpful to keep some type of spiritual journal or diary. It is helpful to look back on things God has shown us or spoken to us. I recommend recording things in it periodically as you have something to say. When I try to do it daily, it often becomes a chore without meaning, and I give up in discouragement.

You may find you want to break up these various aspects of the devotional life, doing some in the morning and some in the evening. There is no set formula. They are tools to help us grow and develop in our walk with God.

Don't give up!

Dr Paul Yonggi Cho says, 'You can teach what you know, but you'll reproduce what you are.' We become what we are in our quiet times with the Father—that's why they are so important. You may find it hard to 'build' in this area, to become disciplined, to use your time well. Join the crowd! Don't accept defeat or failure. Confess to the Lord where you've blown it, and start again. Don't dwell on the past. Pick up the pieces and begin anew. The God of the present doesn't hold our past mistakes against us. He forgives and forgets. We're the ones who remember! 'The men who try to do something and fail are infinitely better than those who try to do nothing and succeed.'

If learning to be organized and to manage your time in your devotional life goes well for a while and then breaks down—regularly—ask God what he may be trying to show you. Perhaps there is a special lesson you need to learn personally in the use of your time. Ask your friends to see if they know why. See if there is some common denominator you've overlooked. It is often easier to be disciplined when you're accountable to someone in this area of personal devotion. Maybe you need a prayer partner or someone you talk to regularly to discuss how it's going. Don't be afraid to ask a brother or sister in Christ to support and help you in this way.

We need to take time to build a spiritual foundation in our lives. All else flows from it. 'The man who walks with God always gets to his destination.' No matter where we're going in life or what we have to do, as Christians we must start with our relationship with the Lord. When we have a solid, secure relationship with the Lord it gives us a foundation to build on in every aspect of life, including our marriages—an area we'll look at next.

3
A Time for Marriage

'A time to embrace and a time to refrain' (Ecclesiastes 3:5).

God speaks very clearly in his word that we are to manage our own households well (1 Tim 3:12). This command cannot be taken lightly. The disease of broken marriages in the body of Christ is running at epidemic level. None of us is immune to this plague. It is easy in the busyness and fulfilment of our Christian lives to neglect our marriages. We must take time to keep them healthy. Some of us may even need a recommitment of our wedding vows to one another. We must look afresh at our marriages and put in the necessary planning and effort to make them fitting examples of what God intended. God may need to interrupt some of the self-destructive lifestyles we've established in order to give us a fresh opportunity to change imbalance into priorities.

I recently read an article in *Good Housekeeping* Magazine (Amercian edition) which listed the ten most important things in a marriage:

> (1) Love
> (2) Laughter

(3) Talk
(4) Involvement
(5) Friendship
(6) Integrity
(7) Tolerance
(8) Adaptability
(9) Sex
(10) Sharing

All of these are 'musts' for every marriage—vital ingredients to the husband-wife relationship. For the Christian marriage I'd add one more—prayer. This must be a foundation stone in our marriage just as it is in our personal life.

Good marriages, however, don't just 'happen'. They take hard work—and lots of it! They take time. Someone has said that 'the best way to keep your marriage safe is not to forget the combination.' The right combination involves planning time to make sure all the vital parts listed above are included in the relationship.

For my husband, Floyd, and me that means planning our schedules together as I mentioned in chapter 1. Our marriage takes priority over all other relationships—except our individual walks with the Lord. It is very easy, though, for the pressures of everything else to squeeze out our time together. We find it necessary to plan in times for our relationship weeks or months in advance in order to make sure our priorities are in balance. When we plan our schedules together we can avoid 'surprises' that we didn't know about. There's also usually time to make adjustments if our planning is unbalanced or if we're not keeping our priorities. We can often adjust to do things together instead of going our separate ways. We can work to make our schedules overlap as much as possible.

I find it important to be flexible as well. I need to plan for the unexpected. Being detailed and organized makes this difficult at times, but it's very important. I never know when Floyd is going to walk in the door and suggest we do something unplanned. I don't want to miss the fun and opportunity of that. Spontaneity is part of the life of any relationship, but we can't just rely on that alone. Careful planning must also be a part.

When our marriages do not function correctly, it throws everything else out of balance. We sometimes need 'quantity' time in order to have 'quality' of relationship. Don't be reluctant to plan in the quantity when it is needed. Everything else will flow more smoothly because we have corrected our priorities.

Adjusting our expectations

Any planning we do for spending time together working on the vital ingredients of a good marriage should include an honest discussion of our individual expectations. We often misunderstand one another because we don't know what our partner is expecting. Of course we must also be willing to make adjustments along the way. Frequently our expectations are totally unrealistic.

When Floyd and I were newly married I had my own clear idea of what a 'perfect' marriage should be like. It included constant harmony and no disagreeing. Unfortunately Floyd and I were too human to live up to that ideal. We had to have a very open discussion of our expectations and whether or not they were realistic. Mine weren't! I had to make some very strategic adjustments.

I once saw an article on marriage called 'Marriage Licence—a Learner's Permit'. Just as we have to learn to drive a car, so we have to learn to guide our marriages. We may have to turn a little to the right or left to avoid some bumps, and we may need to slow down to keep us from crashing. Divorce courts are filled with couples who haven't learned to make the necessary adjustments.

Being together

Marriage is more than romantic feelings. In fact, research has shown that romance diminishes by 80% in the first two years of marriage. Romance should continue to be a part of any marriage, but it is certainly not all there is to it. We must plan for time together to grow in our relationship and understanding of one another. Time spent being together is an investment—there are rich dividends from it.

It is important to look for ways in which our time can overlap in our daily and weekly schedules. We need to plan for evenings out, for fun and for weekends off as well as looking for ways to share our work, our ministry and our household duties together. We need to do things together. This is sometimes called 'aesthetic intimacy'—sharing experiences, 'tasting' things together, mutually appreciating life.

Floyd and I often plan in enough time to walk together to our various meetings or appointments. We use that time to talk and share together. The exercise is great too! You might find it enjoyable to cook a meal together and talk as you work, or do the weekly shopping as a team. I read one article about a pastor's wife who described her marriage as a 'marriage on wheels'. Her time together with her busy husband was scarce. One day she had an idea. She suddenly realized how much time he spent behind the wheel of the car visiting members of their congregation, so she decided to be with him in the car. With no phone or doorbell to intrude, they had plenty of opportunity for peace, privacy and growth in their relationship. She took along little things to do while her husband made pastoral visits and ran errands for the church. When children came along, she took toys, books and games to keep them occupied as well. A very creative solution to finding time together.

Another couple I read about started planning a weekly 'date for fun'. They kept one lunchtime a week to do something special (and fun) together. One week they went to the park with a picnic lunch and a kite. Another time they fed the ducks on the local pond. They also visited museums, went bowling, rode a motorbike and had lots of laughs looking at their old photo albums. Every week the church staff could hardly wait to hear what the pastor and his wife had done that week!

Floyd and I often can't be together because of his busy travel schedule. Something I like to do is send cards ahead to greet him at his various destinations. In this way we can be together even while we're apart. I also have a special little bank where I regularly put some of my loose change to save for doing special things together when he is home. It's amazing how quickly the coins add up. We've enjoyed some very special times together thanks to that little bank.

It is easy to become so busy with outside interests that we begin to take each other for granted. When we do this we don't take the needed time to be together that nourishes our relationship. I once had someone tell me that spending time together with our marriage partner was 'an extravagant waste of time'. If so, it's a necessary extravagance!

Friendship

Marriage must be built on friendship. We should be each other's closest and best friend. We cannot take this friendship for granted; it must be worked at and developed. It's not so much what we can *do* for each other that we need—it is each other . . . as friends. For some couples the friendship comes easily, for others it must be worked at. Again, that takes time—time that we must make room for in our schedule.

To have quality friendship there must be freedom to be ourselves, freedom to be open and honest, and freedom to share everything. That freedom can only exist when there is trust, security and confidence in the marriage relationship. Floyd and I both lead very full and busy lives. Neither of us ever have to puzzle over how to fill up our time. There's always more to fill up our days than there are hours in the day. Years ago, however, Floyd made it clear to me that our relationship is a priority for him. He gave me the freedom to call upon him any time I needed him—even if that meant interrupting a meeting or appointment. His saying that gave me such security and confidence. I've only had to do that once, but I know I'm free to do it if the need ever arises. If a wife knows she is more important than her husband's job, she can handle almost anything.

Sensitivity towards one another is a very important part of friendship. I recently went through several weeks of very trying and difficult situations. I found myself crying a lot and feeling extremely vulnerable. Floyd had been away for most of this period, but when he came home he immediately sensed what I had been going through. He put my coat on, lead me out of the door, and took me shopping for a special little love gift to encourage me. He's a very generous husband and has bought me many gifts through the years of our marriage, but this one was special. Not because of what it was, but because of the sensitivity it reflected. It didn't take a lot of time, but I still feel the 'glow' of his love and care in response to my need.

If our friendship is not what it should be, our relationship begins to break down and we start to drift apart. There are signals we can watch for that tell us to be on guard:

▷ Loss of good, deep communication.

▷ Priorities are not being fulfilled (personal devotions, praying together, time with the family, etc).

▷ Failure to keep things in perspective—God, family, others.

▷ Failure to understand each other's needs—and respond properly to them.

▷ Stubborn silence.

▷ Sarcastic comments, 'digs', public ridicule.

▷ Breakdown of sexual relationship.

▷ Spending less and less time at home.

If any of these start to show up, we must take time out for our friendship and marriage relationship—it's crucial!

Friendship in our marriages is a wonderful gift, and we must treasure it. We must both work at the friendship to keep it growing. We must take the time necessary for that. As we do, our joys are doubled and our burdens are halved.

Communication

One of the signals of couples drifting apart is loss of good communication. In the midst of busyness we may not keep our communication in the place of priority it should be. Communication is the 'life-line' of the marriage relationship—the soul, the means by which the relationship is sustained. When we spend time with God, we listen to the most important voice in heaven. When we spend time talking with our partner, we listen to the most important voice on earth. This is vital for both partners, but especially for the wife. A husband must be careful to take time to meet this need in his wife. He can never just assume she is aware of things. 'Assumption is the mother of all confusion'—simple communication can save a lot of problems. Wives must give up their 'right to know'. A wife needs to trust her husband to communicate—and trust the Lord to speak to him to do that. She can't demand.

Floyd and I have found it helpful to have little daily 'debriefing' times. They don't need to be long, but they should be consistent. It helps us to stay in touch with one another. He tells me a little about his day—things he did, people he saw, points of interest to me—and I tell him about mine. It keeps us from piling up a big backlog of things we've not been able to tell each other. One of the systems we've used in our marriage is making little lists of things we want to be sure to tell one another. We usually can't do it right away, but we don't want to forget. We make a note of it and keep a running list of things to share when we do have the moments together to do that. This is a simple system that helps to ensure we don't forget to communicate the things we should.

Timing is important in communication. Sensitive issues should not be discussed late at night when you're both tired—unless you are both late night people. Plan a time earlier in the day for sharing these things. But if you have young children who are noisy and constantly demanding, clearly the evening is going to be the best time for you. But don't leave it too late! We're not mind-readers in our marriages, even

45

though we may know one another well. Communication gives our partners the opportunity to see inside us. We create a 'word-window' for them to see inside us. Taking the quantity of time that is needed for this type of communication brings that 'quality' into our relationship that is so invaluable.

Disagreeing

Conflict does not make a marriage good or bad—it is how we deal with it that is important. If not dealt with properly, it can destroy even the best of marriages. Learning how to disagree is a vital part of communication.

Ephesians 4:26–27 tells us, 'Do not let the sun go down while you are still angry, and do not give the devil a foothold.' We need to be careful that we do not store up our disagreements. When we were newly married, because of my idea of a 'perfect' marriage, I wouldn't express any disagreements to Floyd. Instead I bottled them up inside and carried them around with me. After we'd been married about six months, that internal bottle exploded because it was so full—at 2.00 a.m.! We talked through the night until we'd worked out what had happened and resolved our areas of conflict. It would have been much easier for both of us if I had dealt with the problems as they arose, 'before the sun went down'.

There are some practical guidelines we can follow on how to disagree. They're what I call 'rules for fair fighting!'

▷ Define the issue. Is it worth disagreeing over?

▷ Wait until you're less emotional. A few hours can help you see things in their proper perspective.

▷ Pray—get your attitude right.

▷ It may help to 'walk and talk'. A change of scenery can help to dissolve the tension.

▷ After you've disagreed, it may help to be with other people before you try to sort things out. Your emotions can settle down a little then.

▷ Wait until you're alone. Your friends won't be too keen on being caught up in a quarrel.

▷ Listen. Hear your partner out.

▷ Don't try to work out a problem late at night when you're tired.

▷ Don't argue when you're hungry. You're even more susceptible to irritation.

▷ Wait until your children are elsewhere. You don't want them getting involved and taking sides.

▷ Make sure you have enough time. Don't try to 'squeeze it in'.

▷ See it through. Don't stop in the middle.

▷ Be polite and kind. Watch your tone of voice. Don't interrupt. Don't raise your voice.

▷ Stay calm. Maintain self-control. Don't say things you'll regret later.

▷ Try to see the matter from the other person's view.

▷ Talk things through until you reach a point of understanding, even if you can't come to an agreement.

▷ Stick to the subject.

▷ Stick to the facts.

▷ If you're wrong, concede graciously.

I've heard it said, 'Where two people agree on everything, one of them is unnecessary.' We're meant to complement each other—to balance one another. We don't need to be alike or think alike. We need to take time to talk and learn from one another. If we do disagree, we need to resolve our disagreement in a Christlike manner.

Freedom to change

We must not look upon marriage as a fixed entity. Not only do our ideas about marriage change over the course of the years, but we as people change. The surest way to be unhappy in our relationship is to expect our marriage (and our partner) to remain the same for ever. If we are fixed on an image of the past or on the way we think things should be, we'll feel threatened every time our partner seems to change. We need to give one another freedom and room to grow.

Someone was asked what makes a marriage stay a marriage? The person wisely replied that 'it takes a loose rein to keep a marriage tight'. He went on to explain that although he had been married to the same woman for many years, he had had four or five wives during that time. His wife had changed a lot through the course of their marriage. She was one person, but she had become another as she learned and matured. Changing and becoming. That's what most of us are about, especially as Christians. Change is what truly characterizes all of us, both men and women. Our love and commitment remain the same, but their outworking changes through the years. We must give one another time and space for this change to take place.

I heard an old quote that said, 'Marriage is like strong horseradish. You can praise it and still have tears in your eyes.' Marriage has its ups and downs, but it's still a wonderful gift from the Lord to us as Christian couples. In our marriages we need to give each other comfort, warmth and counsel. We need to have fun and laugh together. There may be areas we need to take to the cross. We may need to give up our rights and receive grace anew to be all God wants us to be in our relationships. The friendship we have developed with the Lord will enable us to be a better wife, husband, friend, counsellor and help-mate. We need to take time to embrace our marriages to see them work effectively and grow. A healthy marriage paves the way for a loving family.

4

A Time for Family

'A time to love and a time to hate' (Ecclesiastes 3:8).

Our families are important. In the day and age in which we live they are under attack. Traditional structures and values are changing. We must guard our families and take time for them or they will cease to be the precious little community God intended them to be.

We often plan for the family last, but it should be first. The situation is similar to that of marriage: a good family won't just happen—we have to make time for it. Good families aren't born—they're made. Being a good family isn't dependent on money, material possessions, education or careers. We make them what they are—good or bad. We must spend time together in our families in order to develop them into all God wants . . . even if it's a little stiff and forced to begin with. We must take time for the family. And we must protect that time once it's planned so that it doesn't get eaten away.

Time with our children, with our families, isn't wasted time, it's some of the most important time we'll ever spend. So it shouldn't just be 'squeezed in', but planned for carefully and diligently. I like the point made by this simple little poem:

> Cleaning and dusting will wait
> till tomorrow,
> But babies grow up, I've learned
> to my sorrow.
> So quiet down cobwebs, dust go to
> sleep.
> I'm rocking my baby, and babies
> don't keep.

Our work will keep. Our ministry will keep. Certainly they're important—of eternal value even—but what have we gained if we achieve success but lose our family? Our kids grow up all too quickly, leave home, and begin to make their own lives and families. We have a limited amount of time to have input into their lives, and shouldn't miss that opportunity.

At the end of last year my husband was looking over his schedule for the year ahead. As he had planned his engagements for the year, he hadn't been aware of how quickly his time had filled up and how much of it would be spent away from home. As he looked at it he realized it was too full and he was away too often. So he totally re-did his schedule for the year. It wasn't easy, but it was getting his priorities back in their right place. I admired him for it. Our children are in their crucial teenage years now. They need him around more than ever before. Putting our family first may require this kind of critical evaluation and restructuring.

Our children need both parents. It's easy to think of bringing up children as primarily the mother's role, but that isn't a biblical picture. Our kids need both Mum and Dad. In fact, they need their father increasingly as they get older. Floyd has a wonderful and very special relationship with our daughter, Misha. He's her hero and she's the apple of his eye, his 'angel'. They're warm, loving and affectionate in their friendship. I remember someone telling Floyd that someday Misha's husband would thank him for the friendship he had developed with her. This friendship is not only important for the present, it is also building a foundation for her future relationship with her husband.

It takes a special formula or recipe to put a good family together. You have to have all the right ingredients. Let's look at some of those very special and important ingredients for putting together the kind of family God wants us to have. Each ingredient needs time and attention in order for the recipe to be successful.

Commitment

A good family is not without problems, but it has learned how to pull together to meet the challenge of those problems. It has learned how to help one another in going through difficulty. That takes commitment. One of the greatest needs we all have is to feel secure and have a good sense of self-esteem. This is something that needs to be developed in the home. We need to affirm one another's strengths and not just focus on our weaknesses. We need to express thankfulness as often as correction. Research has shown that children are rebuked and corrected seven times more than they are encouraged. We need to affirm our children for who they are, not just for what they do. We need to develop their self-worth.

One of the ways we can do this is by expressing appreciation. The need to feel appreciated is one of the deepest human needs. We should express it to one another and in front of others. We should do it for small things as well as big things. Expressing appreciation helps each member of the family grow and flourish. It's like watering a plant and watching it grow. We should be generous with our praise and stingy with blame.

We should also endeavour to be affectionate. Expressing love is a way to 'raise positive kids in a negative world'. We should take the opportunity to hug, hold hands, etc. There are three levels on which we can express love:

▷ touch—hugging, kissing or holding our children; wrestling and playing with them.

▷ speaking—expressing our love verbally.

▷ showing—an attitude of love and warmth—letting our child know that no matter what he does, we'll never stop loving him; taking time to 'refuel' our children in the home.

For some of us, expressing our love, and especially being affectionate, may not be easy. We may not have had that experience ourselves as children. We may be reserved. We may feel uncomfortable in doing it. Whatever the barriers, we must work at overcoming them.

In a strong family the members are dedicated to promoting each other's welfare and happiness. They stick together through good and bad. They love and support each other. They're loyal. They're a team. They pull together. Each family team is part of a bigger family. It's important to include the extended family, even if this is difficult and they are far away. We have a lovely 'photo wall' in our home where we have photos of our family members who are scattered all around the world. It is in a prominent place where we can all see it often, helping to remind us of the bigger team we're separated from by many miles. The phone, of course, can also keep us in touch. It's worth the expense. When Floyd's parents retired after forty years of pastoral ministry, they joined us in our work in Amsterdam. They often say they didn't retire, they simply 'retreaded'! We had the privilege of living near them for five years. It was so wonderful to have grandparents close by for our children. Our extended family can invest much in our smaller family through the richness of their lives. We must make time to keep them a part of us.

The family helps one another—with domestic jobs, personal interests and outside activities. We're involved in one another's lives. We don't just live unto ourselves, but we take time to share in the interests of one another. As our children grow up, we stand increasingly beside them—not over them.

In the family we help prepare our children for life. We try to equip them for the things they will face. We endeavour to teach them principles that will guide them in making decisions for their own lives. One of the things we've worked on with our children is handling money. We've taught them about sharing, being generous, and about faith. When we've given them an allowance, we've had them work up a budget on how they will spend it. Then we've discussed their decisions. When we moved into a new apartment, we encouraged them to take individual steps of faith in trusting God for provision while as a family we were collectively trusting the Lord for our home. It was wonderful to see how the Lord answered their prayers. They were each able to save the money to buy their own beds. Far beyond that, however, was the faith that was cultivated in their hearts through the experience.

In the midst of the family situation, we must allow

room for individual growth. There must be room for each member to be his own person. In our family we have some delightful contrasts. It makes life interesting—and beautiful. We must ensure privacy—and respect it. As our children grow up they need to have areas of their life (and rooms) that are theirs alone. We should respect that and not snoop on each other. We should knock when we enter their rooms. We give space to one another in this way, and we also teach courtesy that extends to others outside our family as well.

Friendship

Within our family units we should be friends. Some families only tolerate one another. I find that so sad. God intended our lives to be closely interwoven and supportive to each other. The friendship relationship starts early. We have to work at developing that friendship. If we want to be friends with our children when they become adults, it starts when they are babies and toddlers. From a very early age, my daughter and I had little tea-times together. The occasional ten to fifteen minutes together goes a long way. Now that she's older, we have one evening a week that we reserve to go out shopping and have fun together. We do our best to make sure nothing gets in the way of our weekly appointment.

We need to learn to enjoy, not just endure, each other's presence. We can change the world by starting inside our home. We learn and grow as we develop friendships within our own families.

Communication

Communication builds friendship. Loss of it signals

breakdown in the family. A strong family will spend lots of time in conversation. They will sit down and have family discussions. We often do this in our family, especially when we have differing opinions about things. We learn from each other, and we come to mutual conclusions about things we are facing together.

Much is accomplished by communication. Through it comes hope when we're discouraged; comfort when we're hurt; counsel when we need wisdom; stimulus when we are stagnant; and refreshment when we are dry. We need to believe that each member has something important to say—and they do. Recently, Floyd was interviewed on television on the topic of trends. Before he left for this he sat down with our daughter, Misha, and discussed what he should say. It was lovely to watch the programme later and hear him quoting her. She had some major insights to contribute.

We must take time to work on improving communication in our family. One of the ways we can do this is by providing an atmosphere of communication. This can be done by encouraging one another to share; by making ourselves available; by being careful not to 'talk down' to one another; respecting one another; by sharing what we've learned; by listening; and by extending trust. The last two are very important.

Sometimes we find it hard just to listen. Remember, we don't always have to have the right answers. Sometimes the only thing needed in communication is a listening ear. There are times when we don't understand ourselves. We want someone to listen and try to help us understand. We need to listen and learn to 'read between the lines'. We need to ask the right questions. We need to listen and think like a kid.

We also need to trust. Our children will respond to

that trust and rise to the challenge it brings. We need
to expect the best instead of fearing the worst. Trusting
also helps to develop that self-worth and self-
confidence we spoke of earlier.

Communication involves taking time to answer
questions. We positively need to encourage and give
the freedom to ask questions. We can encourage open
communication through our words, by having an
understanding ear, through affection, and by thoughtful, loving acts. You may find it helpful to keep a chart
for a while to evaluate your family communication.
How much quality time do you spend listening and
talking to each member in your family? Recent studies
have shown that most fathers have less than three
minutes each day of eye-to-eye contact with their
children. My children sometimes joke with their dad,
saying they haven't had their three minutes yet.

As part of effective communication, we need to
show openness and vulnerability before our children.
We need to show them we're human too. After all,
they see our faults and weaknesses anyway. As we're
honest with them, it helps them to be open themselves. We must be quick and willing to say, 'I'm sorry,
I was wrong.' It is very hard to say this at times, but it
is so important. It sets an example for them. We must
forgive each family member when they're wrong, even
when we've been hurt. God doesn't hold grudges, and
we shouldn't either.

We must include time to talk about small, trivial
things as well as the deep issues of life. Our children
will never feel free to talk to us about drugs, sex and
other major things they're facing if they can't talk
to us about cars, clothes, computers and make-up.

The sex education of our children belongs in our
home. Don't say or think that what they don't know
won't hurt them. Trying to keep our children innocent

by keeping them ignorant won't work. They're going to learn about sex sooner or later, so we need to teach them from a Christian perspective as soon as possible. We can't leave this vital part of their growth and development to their friends, their teachers, or even to the church. Mum and Dad need to take an active role in this aspect of communication.

All these vital areas of communication *must* be planned. As has already been pointed out, they won't just happen. We plan what we call 'family times'. We usually have this time at least once a week. It's a bit of a trick to get it together at times because of co-ordinating everyone's schedules, but it can be done. We have devotions, discuss issues and questions, and make family decisions and plans for other activities. Clearly, such times must be suited to the current ages of your children, and developed as time goes on.

When our children were babies, we started the nightly ritual of tucking them in at bed-time. We've modified this somewhat as they've grown up, but we still have a bed-time ritual. It's an important time to tell our children we love them and to pray with them. It only takes a few minutes, but they're valuable minutes. It's often during these times that they share things that are on their hearts.

We need to assist our children with their problems and help them deal with their fears. We can't shelter our children, but we can help them learn how to deal with these things and cope with them. With their hurts, we teach them to forgive. With their sins, we show them how to repent. With their fears, we help them face them—being careful not to make light of them.

Do good, strong families quarrel? Is that part of their communication? Yes, of course—they're human. We must learn how to deal with conflict in a positive way.

We must learn to 'fight fair'; we must talk openly; we must discuss things and learn to compromise. We will only be prepared for disagreements outside the home when we can deal properly with those within.

Meal-times

If we don't take meal-times seriously we can miss out on a daily opportunity to build sound family relationships. We need to begin the day together as a family. We find this requires a little give and take on the part of each one. Some have to get up a little earlier and some have to move a little more quickly to get off on time. It's important to start the day together even if it's only for a few minutes.

Meal-times are an important part of family life, a part that is becoming increasingly rare in our day and age. A number of factors are involved in bringing the family all together around the table. These include being willing to wait for the others to get home, and having an unrushed meal in order to make the time really effective.

The meal-time should bring everyone together. It's a time for fellowship and socializing, for sharing our lives (encourage that sharing), asking questions, and developing the art of conversation. I remember one mother telling me how hard it was to get her quiet son involved in conversation. She finally got through to him when she compared it to a ball game. 'Someone throws you a ball,' she explained, 'and you have to pick it up and throw it back.' Meal-times become a learning time for things like this. It's also a time for training in areas such as manners and etiquette—we practice good manners and learn from our mistakes. It's a time to involve our children in hospitality—we learn to welcome guests into our family and serve them.

We can set the atmosphere for what I call 'meaningful meal-times'. A nicely set table, food served attractively and creatively, and effort put into good communication can make our times around the table opportunities to deepen our family relationships. When our children were small, we often clapped at the end of the meal for the cook. They learned to express gratitude and appreciation while encouraging Mum. Taking time to thank God for this provision for us is also an important part of expressing gratitude at mealtimes. In fact, in Holland where we live they pray twice. They bless the food before, and thank the Lord for it afterwards.

We also need to take time to develop traditions in our families, a lot of which can take place around the meal table. Traditions give security and continuity. Certain meals, special holidays, and various events become a part of our individual family heritage through the traditions we set. They strengthen our family bonds. I learned how important this is one year at Christmas. I had been away at a conference and returned just a few days before Christmas. Because of limited time, I suggested that we didn't do some of our usual things but took a few shortcuts to save time. My children almost left home! They couldn't imagine how I could possibly not decorate the whole house, put all our favourite and special ornaments out, hang up our stockings, and put our ragged-looking angel on top of the tree. These (and many other things) were part of who we are as a family and how we express ourselves at this particular festive season. It gave them security and a sense of continuity.

We need to share our family heritage with our children. Misha and Matthew love to hear things from when Mum and Dad were kids. We have a unique little book of drawings of escapades from Floyd's childhood that we love to share with guests in our home. Our children also like to hear stories from our early days in Youth With A Mission. Stories of how God 'healed' a leaky air mattress, saved a criminal, and multiplied our mosquito repellent, never grow old!

Time together

We need to be sure to do things with our children and not just for them. In recent years there seems to have been a running debate over which is more important—quantity time or quality time. In a good family, quantity and quality go hand in hand. Time spent together should be good time. No one enjoys hours of arguing or bickering. Time together needs to be sufficient and adequate. A quality relationship cannot be developed in a few minutes.

The list of ideas for spending time together is endless. A whole book could be written on that topic alone. We'll look here at just a few areas to stimulate your imagination over the variety of activities you can be involved in together.

▷ Organized fun: camping, cycling, walks, sports, picnics, going to the pictures, museums, concerts, etc.

▷ Reading together: this item is high on my list of family activities. We started reading together when our children were infants. In the morning we would read together and have a family devotional time. We used this time to discuss and teach things that helped shape our views as a Christian family. In the evening we read entertaining and amusing things together as a family. Although our children are different ages, we tried to read things that would reach all levels. Two of our favourites were *The Little House on the Prairie* series and the *Narnia* series. By our example and through our reading together, we wanted to develop a love for literature. There are times when I think we may have done too good a job—our children devour books; their rooms are filled with them!

It is important to create an appreciation for a variety of literature as well as for current events. This means investing in good materials—books, poems, regular visits to the local library, and borrowing books. In our home we've been surrounded by good literature and it has certainly paid off. Our son, Matthew, loves to write. He writes short stories, books, and film scripts. Our daughter, Misha, draws and writes poems. I love the flow of creativity within them and feel I've had a part in that as their mother in the way I've helped to guide and inspire them through the many hours we spent reading together.

Floyd also created his own stories for our children. When we lived in the heart of the red light district here in Amsterdam across the street from the Oude Kerk (old church), he told the children a series of stories about Peter the church mouse. We also had tales about a bunch of interesting underwater creatures. There was Wally the Whale, Sammy the Shark (the baddy), Billy Bass (the evangelist), and many others. We loved these stories. My only regret is that we didn't tape them.

▷ Days off and family holidays: these have to be planned and protected from being squeezed out and cancelled. Urgent and important matters always come up, but very few are of such priority to mean cancellation of family events.

We should plan activities that everyone will enjoy. It's easy just to go our separate ways. There are times, of course, when this will happen, but we mustn't let it happen all the time or our family life will disintegrate.

We save money for our family activities so that we can do special things together. The children, too, help earn money for our family outings.

You can learn something new together on days off. You can plan a project everyone can have a part in. You can have things available in the home that will encourage mixing in together—a puzzle sitting out on a table, games, etc.

▷ Inspire creativity: we all have four basic human needs—to be loved, to feel secure, to feel successful, and to be creative. We can work at developing creativity in our children. We can encourage it, help them, and do creative things with them. We can make things together as a family. We can also work at developing the individual gifts and abilities God has placed in their lives by providing materials for the expression of those gifts, by praising their efforts, and by helping them get instruction to further their gifts.

▷ Travel: because Floyd travels a lot, we have found it a wonderful family activity for each of the children to go with him at times. This gives an opportunity for time alone with him, but, even more important, it gives them a better understanding of what he does when he is away from home. They feel more a part of it, and they know how to pray for him when he's away.

It's fun to take special trips together as a family—even short ones. You can think of ways to learn

together as you travel. Travelling helps to develop
flexibility in children. Our children have had to
learn to be flexible through the years because of our
unusual lifestyle. I find it amazing when I see
families who are completely upset by the least little
change in routine or activity. Change is a major
feature of the modern world—we need to prepare
our children for it.

Travelling together also gives us the opportunity
to accept those who are different from us—another
important concept for our children to learn.

▷ Events: celebrations for the unexpected, the special,
the silly and the fun are wonderful family activities.
'I love Daddy' parties, 'Thank you for the sun'
parties (a very special one in rainy Holland!), a 'first
tooth out' party, a 'kiss and tickle party', a 'good
report-card' party, 'the first day of spring party'—
well, do you get the idea? We overlook countless
things that we *could* celebrate—things that make
family events.

Spiritual health

This has already been mentioned in a variety of ways,
but it certainly bears repeating. We help create a
spiritual foundation in the lives of our children
through the things we do together as a family.
Devotional times are essential—it is here that we teach
and disciple our children. We learn from them, too,
not just them from us. I've learned so much from my
children. They've helped me see many areas of weakness and need in my own life. They've also given me
wonderful sermon illustrations!

We must be faithful in teaching our children sound
Christian principles. We must explain why things

should or shouldn't be done—and not just give them a list of do's and don'ts. The principles we instil in them will help to guide them long after Mum and Dad can no longer be there beside them.

Praying together is another vital part of our spiritual health as a family. It is good to record our family prayers and the answers to them in some sort of prayer diary. It builds faith to see how God has answered. We need to include our children in praying for family needs. Don't be afraid to share with them. Our children need to be a part of seeking God for guidance and lifting up our family needs to him. 'Out of the mouths of babes' God will often speak.

As you've read through this chapter, you may have felt guilty over how you've developed your own family life. You may be thinking it's hopeless or it's too late. It's never too late to begin. Weak families *can* be made strong . . . step by step with continual effort. This does require an investment of time and energy, but the cost isn't too high. It is an investment in the future for all of us—and it is the best investment we'll ever make.

Our relationships in the home help prepare us for friendships with others. We must focus time and attention on the people God brings into our lives, as we'll see in the following chapter.

5
A Time for Friendship

'A time to tear and a time to mend, a time to be silent and a time to speak' (Ecclesiastes 3:7).

'Never plan for an hour's work to be done in an hour.' Have you heard that one before? How many times do we get frustrated because we can't accomplish a task in the time we have allotted for it? We overschedule. We need to leave room for the unexpected—the interruptions that come along. We should learn to be flexible. True, we must establish priorities. We must find the Lord's perspective on our schedule and then endeavour to stick to it. But that should always be balanced with being flexible and open. It's a tricky tight-rope at times. But our schedule should never be a bondage, it should always be a tool.

There will always be the unexpected. Indeed, the unexpected is often part of God's plan. One pastor calls this the 'theology of interrupting'. We must keep a concrete awareness that even when there are many interruptions, the Lord gives grace to carry us through and keep things in balance and in line with our priorities. He may even be bringing a blessing our way. And we wouldn't want to miss anything God has for us. James 1:2 says (in J. B. Phillips' rendering): 'When all kinds of trials and temptations crowd into your lives, my brothers, don't resent them as intruders, but welcome them as friends!' In maintaining this kind of flexibility our schedule may have to be totally ignored. This is the balancing side to what I've already said about sticking to our schedule and learning how to say no to interruptions. These two aspects of scheduling and flexibility must always be held in balance. The key link between the two is discernment and sensitivity to the voice of the Spirit to guide us in each situation.

Not every crisis is a crisis. We must continually ask God for wisdom to discern which people and situations need our attention and which don't. The important thing is to be open and free in our spirits to adjustments along the way as the Lord directs. A crisis may hold blessing for us as well. Someone explained that the Chinese character for the word 'crisis' is made up of two parts: one is the symbol for danger, the other is the symbol for opportunity. An unexpected crisis can be an opportunity for growth. God wants us to be flexible and open.

The world is change; time is change; change is a way of life—it always has been and always will be. 'Blessed is the man who has discovered there is nothing permanent in life but change.' We shouldn't become so stuck into a rut of time management that we miss the unexpected that God brings or that we miss being open to change. One particular way in which God brings the unexpected into our lives is in the form of people. People are more important than things. There is the schedule, there is the job that God has given us to do, but people should always come above these tasks. There are times when I have a list of priorities that God has given me for the day and someone comes along unexpectedly. My temptation might be to say, 'What a bother.' Often God has said to me, 'Wait a minute. That person is more important than all those papers on your desk. In fact, I've brought this person here for a special purpose.' At that point I realize I must lay aside my schedule, my papers and my plans and give my attention to this person. We must remain Flexible within a Framework of planing—the two 'F's are the key. We need to be flexible but not limp.

Faster doesn't always mean better—'haste makes waste.' Some time-saving techniques have the potential to destroy relationships and hurt people. People are always more important than schedules. A good schedule is adaptable, not collapsible. God wants to teach us how to flow with change and be flexible. This means a certain amount of availability. We don't have to be available to everybody all the time, but there are those times when God brings people into our lives unexpectedly and we need to be available. However, being available to everybody all the time is poor time management. Again, the important word here is balance.

It helps if we let people know when we are available. Is there a certain time of day or particular day of the week when you are available? Letting people know when we are available gives us a sense of security and freedom. In Amsterdam, we have one day a week for our regular leaders' meeting. During the day we set aside time when anyone can come who has a need for prayer, a question they want to ask, a problem they want to discuss, or a suggestion they want to make to the leaders. Anyone can come with anything, because we're available. This has been very helpful in a large community that is spread out over the whole city. It is not always convenient for someone to 'drop in' and speak to one of the leaders, but our staff know they can come during this open time.

In managing our time, the word 'people' can take on rather a negative ring. This is especially true in town life where so many people are around all the time. We begin to think of people as a pressure or a bother or a hindrance. Or maybe we spiritualize it a bit and consider them an 'attack of the Enemy'. But none of these is God's perspective. People often use one another to achieve something they want, but God's way is that we should be a blessing and a gift to one another. The Lord gives many good gifts to us, the most precious being his Son, Jesus Christ a friend who sticks closer than a brother. Next to the Son and the Spirit, one of the most wonderful gifts God has given us is the gift we are to one another in the body of Christ.

Friends are a gift

One of the ways we are a gift to each other is in the area of friendship. God may interrupt our schedule with people in order to build friendships. We're often unaware of this, or we don't think we need such friendships, or we simply don't want to take the time for them. God intends our lives as Christians to be interwoven—he wants us to be linked into one another. We must make room and time in our lives for the friendships God has for us.

I once received a note from a friend with this message on it:

A friend – strengthens the heart
        – repairs the hurt
        – encourages the discovery
        – enlightens the mind
        – dissolves the pain
        – banishes the loneliness
        – understands the anxiety

- increases the joy
- deepens the spirit
- frees the soul

That's a pretty tall order! I believe, however, that it captures the essence of what God intends friendship to be. Proverbs 17:17 tells us that 'a friend loves at all times'. That sums it up nicely.

We all need friends. We need the love that comes through friendship. Love is a basic human need. We all need it—no matter how self-sufficient, 'macho', wealthy or successful we may be. If we want this love and want friends, we must show ourselves friendly. Sometimes we struggle in this area of friendship. We say we're shy—we can't reach out to others. But we shouldn't use shyness as an excuse. People often find it hard to believe that I am basically a shy person. Floyd has always been the outgoing one in our relationship. Shyness was something I had to over-come. It was—and still is—much easier for me to sit back and listen to others. But years ago the Lord challenged me that I would never be all that he wanted me to be if I used shyness as an excuse. I chose to step out of my shyness and quietness. It was hard at first. I was scared. I was nervous. I was insecure. But the more I took those steps of reaching out to people, the easier it became. If we want friendship, we can't just wait for it to come to us on a plate; we must begin by reaching out to those around us. We must look for those who are lonely. We must *be* a friend to others. In fact, the only way to have a friend is to be one.

Principles of friendship

There are many principles of friendship—far too many to make note of them all here—but it would be good to consider a few. In living or working closely with people there will always be conflicts and tensions. We *must* take time to work through them. If we don't, we won't have quality friendships. Besides that, it will hinder the Lord working in and through our lives and ministries. Conflicts hinder the flow of the Spirit. A very important part of friendship is making time to work through difficulties.

We must learn to 'forbear' one another—have patience towards one another. Part of this is learning to accept one another as we are. If you were to know me personally, there would probably be things you would not like about me. I'm sure there are things I do or don't do that would get on your nerves. My husband, Floyd, sometimes gets frustrated when I talk to him in detail. He likes to hear the 'headlines'. But I think in a detailed way, and so my communication tends to be detailed. I love to share with Floyd all the little things that are so important to me, and because he loves me, he is patient with me when I do this. As friends, we need to forbear each other in our weaknesses and idiosyncrasies.

Some of us struggle with insecurity. We must be careful that we don't let our insecurities rule our actions. We may feel left out by others, or we may feel we don't fit in, so we begin to withdraw from those around us and spend time all alone. This often arises because we feel insecure. We need to assume that others like us. We need to be careful that we do not entertain thoughts of rejection. Satan will use them to discourage us and hinder friendship from developing.

We must also be careful to guard our speech. Gossip is divisive. Proverbs 16:28 says, 'A gossip separates close friends.' Being critical, grumbling, complaining, and negative is deadly. The tongue is a very small member of our body, but its potential impact is huge. It can bring great discord. It can cause people to dislike us, or to avoid us. It can hinder unity. It can crush and destroy. It can be a giant stumbling-block to friendship unless we keep it under control.

Loyalty is another vital ingredient of friendship. If someone shares a confidential matter with us, we must be careful not to share it with someone else. We may think others would benefit from hearing it, but it is not our place to share it. If others share their hearts with us, confess sins to us, or in any way make themselves vulnerable to us, it is because they want to be account-able to someone or they want someone to pray with and support them. We must keep what is shared between the two of us and the Lord. We need to be so careful in this area. God wants openness and sharing in our lives with one another, but it can be destroyed in a few seconds by not maintaining loyalty in that openness.

Having times of prayer together is also important to friendship. Fellowship is wonderful. Joking together and having fun is tremendous. But praying together is the seal of friendship. Prayer solidifies our friendship. It takes it to a level that talking alone cannot reach. We need to make sure that our friendships do not just stay at the talking level, but move on into prayer. We must take time and make time to pray together.

It is important to avoid cliques in our friendships. We must be careful not to get in our own little group and stay there. We should be close but not exclusive. We should never be so 'tight' that others feel neglected or left out. We should reach out to those who are different from us. Get to know people from other countries, backgrounds and churches. God wants to enrich our lives through the variety of people around us. We'll miss so much if we just stay in our own little circle. Reaching out to those who are different from us is not always easy, but it is worth while. I remember how the Lord once prompted me to develop a friendship with a girl who was as different from me as day is from night. I hardly knew where to begin in getting to know her. If I liked black, she liked white. If I wanted to sleep in, she wanted to get up early. It wasn't easy, but I knew God had put it in my heart to become her friend. Our relationship had its ups and downs, but in time we became very close. My life was deeply enriched by hers and vice versa. We need friendships with those of both similar and different interests.

God will give each of us special friendships as we are obedient to him in reaching out to those around us. We must be careful that we don't become jealous of one another's friendships. If we struggle with this, we must ask the Lord to forgive us, and to help us in making our own relationships.

We need each other. Friendship is not an optional extra—we are incomplete without it. We belong to one another in the body of Christ. Someone has said that everybody who belongs to Jesus belongs to everybody who belongs to Jesus! That's a complicated way of saying we belong to one another, but it reminds us that we can't leave Jesus out of the picture. We are a gift from the Lord to each other. Regardless of age, race, beliefs, background, sex, shape or size, we belong to one another in the Christian family. In fact, we must keep in mind that God wants adults to develop friendships with children too. Children have so much to teach us and to give us. If you haven't caught on to that secret, you're missing something very special. I've learned some of my deepest spiritual lessons through children. I'm grateful for that. It's humbling at times, but also very rewarding.

Barriers to friendship

Whenever I speak on the topic of friendship, peopl
immediately begin talking about lack of time. I ca
identify with that because I'm busy too. We often se
time as a big barrier to friendship. Busyness can be
problem, but what are our values? Our friends are a
important part of our life. We must simply *make* time t
develop and deepen our friendships.

However, there are genuine barriers to friendshi
that we must look at now. Envy and jealousy will kill
friendship before it's even begun. Fear can keep u
from stepping out to initiate new relationships. In
security will imprison us in walls of inadequacy.

Disagreements will divide in a split second. Lov
and friendship are of far greater importance than ou
theological positions. Sometimes we need to agree t
disagree. We need the freedom to have different idea
so that we can have true spiritual unity—there can b
unity in our diversity.

Lack of encouragement is a big barrier to friendshi
Although God should be given the glory for what h
has done in our lives, we still need to encourage on
another. Man lives by affirmation and encouragemen
even more than he does by bread. Encouragemen
builds friendship.

Sometimes we don't know how to be open. This ca
hinder our friendships as well. Maybe we haven't ha
teaching on how to build a friendship, or we haven
had it demonstrated to us. Our friends shouldn't b
taken by surprise about things we are doing—we nee
to share personally and openly with them.

Work can be a barrier to friendship. Floyd says wor
is like the poor—it will always be with us. But w
mustn't let it keep us from taking time to build friend
ships.

Friendship is always two-way. If we take without giving back, we will hinder the friendship from growing as it should.

I'm sure there are many more things that can hinder us in developing friendships. The important thing is not to let any of them become a barrier that prohibits friendship. We must look at whatever we have allowed to come into our lives that hinder relationships and remove them so that we can experience all that God has for us. The purpose of friendship is to help one another and build one another up. Proverbs 17:17 says, 'A friend loves at all times, and a brother is born for adversity.' Friendship is a giant reservoir that we need to tap into.

We need to create an environment for fellowship and friendship in our homes, ministries, churches and places of business. We must give one another time and opportunity to develop relationships. Over the years in our ministry in Amsterdam, Floyd and other members of our community have regularly taken time for sports and other forms of physical exercise. It's been great, and not only physically—it has been good for our staff to see that taking time to build relationships and having recreation together is not a sin. We haven't compromised spiritually. This kind of activity is not a way of life—it has to be scheduled in. When we do organize such events, we must be careful not to turn them into prayer meetings. They are for fun and fellowship.

There are different levels of friendship, as we see in the life of Jesus. He spent much time with the twelve disciples. He spent even more time with Peter, James and John. He called John, in particular, the beloved. He couldn't give himself in the same way to everyone, and neither can we. We must commit and submit our friendships to the Lord. We need to have his perspective on those with whom we are to develop a closer relationship.

We must be careful that we don't have false expectations about the nature of our friendships. God's ideas may be different from ours. We can't be everything to everyone, but that shouldn't be an excuse to keep us from developing a close relationship with the few God wants us to get to know well. The priority and commitment of our friendships may change from time to time. That's fine. The friendship can still go on. There are those I've been very close to for a period of time and then our paths have gone in different directions. But the love continues. The next time we see one another we just pick up where we left off.

Practical helps

There are many simple, practical things we can do in taking time for friendship. We live in a world where families are falling apart, where fast food and instant everything is the order of the day. The 'art of keeping in touch' has become a lost art; it has fallen upon hard times. Few have the time or energy to stay in touch with old friends beyond the annual Christmas card with its scribbled promise to do better next year. Many think of friends as something one takes up later in life, along with golf or gardening. Friendship can't be put off until a better time. Like gardening, it requires a high level of maintenance.

The French say, 'To lose a friend is to die a little.' To keep a friend is to add immeasurably to the quality of our life. We need to keep our friendships in constant repair. There are many ways we can do this in a limited amount of time.

There is no such thing as not having time to write something. We often don't keep in touch with friends because we can't do it in a 'perfect' way. Our communication doesn't need to be fancy—it can be simple. The important thing is that it's personal and that we are keeping in touch. A quick note or a postcard with a few scribbled lines will mean a lot to a friend who is longing to hear from us.

I recently read about Eleanor Roosevelt, wife of the famous American president. She was a very active, involved lady, but she managed to keep in touch with her children, grandchildren, godchildren, old friends and new acquaintances through an endless stream of caring, simple, uncomposed notes scribbled on whatever she had at hand—envelopes, menus, hotel laundry lists, the boarding passes of planes. She wasn't concerned about the quality of the prose, she just wrote—'Hope you're doing well . . .' 'I'm on my way to . . .' 'I just saw . . .'

In a drawer in my desk I keep a large supply of notecards, stationery, postcards, etc. They're readily available for me to write quick notes to friends around the world with a short thought or wish I want to communicate. It wasn't always like this. If I couldn't write a long, detailed letter, I wouldn't write at all. One day I realized I'd never have time for all those long letters—short, quick notes were better than nothing. More friends hear from me more often because of this one little change of style. I follow the same policy with thank-you notes to friends. I try to write them as soon after the event or situation as I can. They are just short, quick, simple notes that express my appreciation. I'd often like to write more, but that would mean waiting until I had more time, so I'd probably never get it done! A few loving words of communication work just as well. And, may I also add, it's important to thank people and express appreciation for small things as well as big ones. A loving friendship can begin by letting someone know you appreciate their making coffee for the meeting—or cleaning up afterwards.

Phone calls are in the same category. We often don't make them because we don't have time for a long conversation. I begin many a phone conversation by saying, 'I only have a few minutes . . . but I wanted you to know I was thinking of you today, concerned for you, praying for you.' Three minutes of thoughtful expression in this way can mean an awful lot.

One of my favourite things is sending birthday cards to friends around the world. I send many each month, as well as trying to remember the birthdays of our staff working with us in Amsterdam. It takes a little bit of planning, but not a great deal. I have a birthday book where I keep my main complete list. Once a year I sit down and go through it. I record all the birthdays I want to remember this year in my current agenda. Then once a week I take a few minutes to address cards for the week ahead and get them ready to post. Sometimes I get a bit behind, so then I send a 'late' card. It just takes a little effort, but it helps us keep in touch with those who are dear and special to us around the world.

I also enjoy giving little gifts to people—not expensive things but small tokens of love. It's nice to give them for birthdays and at Christmas, of course, but even more fun is giving them at unexpected times—for encouragement, to say thank you for a job well done, to say, 'I appreciate you.' I have a special shelf in my cupboard where I keep these little gifts on hand, so when the 'need' arises I'm ready to give to someone. I look out for things in the shops. If I see something that 'looks like' someone, I buy it and keep it until the right occasion. I've discovered that God loves to give gifts. (He gives good things to us all the time, doesn't he?) He's faithfully provided through the years for this little way of expressing love and care to those around me.

The Magic of a Friend

It's the little things that matter,
the unexpected things.
The thoughtful gift that gives a lift,
the thrill a phone call brings!

The kindly deed for one in need,
the willingness to share;
The happy smile that helps awhile
and tells someone, 'I care!'

It's the little things that matter,
that adds up in the end
To the priceless, thrilling magic
found only in a friend!

In the day and age in which we live, people are constantly wondering what to invest in—gold? Silver? Art? Real estate? As Christians, we need to invest in people. As we do this, we reap great dividends—love, support, encouragement, fellowship. People are the only thing of real lasting value, and one of the ways we can invest in them is in friendship.

God wants to knit our lives together in friendship—it's one of his most precious gifts to us. He's given us the gift of people, so we need to be careful that we don't miss it. We need the love and objectivity of friends other than our husband or wife. We need to make time and room for these friendships in our lives.

As we give to our husband or wife, our family and friends, we must take time for personal development—or we will have nothing to offer!

6

A Time for Life

'A time to be born and a time to die' (Ecclesiastes 3:2).

When I start planning my time, I usually allocate
time for everything except for myself—for me, Sally, as
a person. I plan for my husband, for my children, for
my friends, but somehow time for myself gets overlooked or squeezed out. I've come to realize that I will
never be the person God wants me to be if I do this. I
need time for me. I need time for personal growth,
learning and development. I need time for personal
refreshment. I need time for personal meditation and
reflection. I need time for life—my life! Time spent on
myself is not wasted time.

In trying to find this time for myself, I've found it
important to look at what are sometimes called 'time
bandits'. There are a lot of things that drain our time
budget, that eat away at the amount of time we have to
work with, and that keeps us from having time for all
the various areas of our lives. In learning to manage
our time effectively, it is important to give attention to
these time-wasters.

We should begin by looking at our schedule very
carefully. As has been said before, it might be helpful

to keep a diary for a week or so. Mark down exactly what you do and how much time you spend doing it. Make this log very detailed and specific. If it takes you five minutes to comb your hair, write that down. Three minutes to brush your teeth, half an hour for a quiet time, fifteen minutes to eat lunch—write down everything you are doing for a number of days and then study it. Prayerfully go over it, asking the Lord to show you things that are eating away at the budget of your time. I think you'll be very surprised at some of the things you see. Ask others to help you as well—someone you work with, your husband or wife, or a close friend. Ask them to help you see 'time bandits' in your life. Their objectivity may well help you to see what can be cut out or what adjustments can be made. I have very much appreciated the times that Floyd has helped me with my schedule. I can easily get bogged down in details, and there are occasions when I waste a lot of my time because of this. I need to get out of the details and focus on the overall picture. I appreciate it when others help me do this.

Also ask other people to help you see how you waste their time! It could be, for example, in the way we communicate or the way we work in areas that overlap with others. We need to learn from each other in this matter. We should write down the fresh solutions we come up with. We could keep a log or a journal. It's important to go over that log from time to time and make sure we are still living up to what God has shown us and what we've learned.

Time bandits

Let's look at some specific time-wasters that keep us from having the personal 'life' time that we all need. One of those mentioned most often in time management is indecision. We are confronted by many different kinds of decision every day. We can go right or left. We can spend five pounds or fifty. We can work with a team or with one person. We can get an outside job or work in our home. We can stay where we are or we can move. We need to ask the Lord to guide us and help us make the right decision, and then act on it. In many situations, any decision is better than none. Sometimes we overspiritualize things far too much. We waste time waiting for lightning to strike from heaven or for the handwriting to appear on the wall when God is expecting us to use the common sense and wisdom that he has given us. In many of our decisions, God wants us to make a choice and move on. In others, obviously, we need to seek him. The key word, again, is balance. We need to be careful that we don't waste time in indecision when we could be moving ahead.

We also need to resist the impulse for unscheduled activities, unless they are really necessary. We may often pray and discern from the Lord our priorities for the day and week. But when something comes along unexpectedly, we may drop all those priorities and give ourselves to this new thing. We spend our time 'putting out fires'. We drop everything to take care of a new, unexpected situation. We lack control. We follow the action rather than leading it, and bow to the tyranny of the urgent. The new thing is usually not of the Lord, but wastes our time and keeps us from what God has already spoken to us about. Far better just to note these new things and then evaluate them later for future involvement. We can, and maybe should, work on them later, but not now.

Along the same line, we shouldn't spring surprises on those we live and work with, for this wastes their time too. We need to communicate our schedule clearly to our husband or wife, with our children, and with those at work. If we don't, it will throw their schedules off with unplanned activities too. I live with a man of vision. He's always getting new thoughts and new ideas. I never know when something is going to come up unexpectedly. I've learned to be flexible, but both of us have learned how to co-ordinate more effectively and not spring surprises on one another.

We need to finish what we start. Our lives often leave a trail of unfinished tasks. Things are usually done better when we see them right through to completion. We also enjoy a sense of satisfaction and fulfilment when we accomplish what God has put before us. How many of us have started a project, reached 50 to 75% along the way, and then set it aside for a while? We walk around feeling guilty and frustrated. We feel like we've blown it. It hangs like a cloud over our heads. Then one day we say, 'This is ridiculous! I've got to get that finished.' And we do. I recently finished a project that I started two years ago. For those two years, it hung like a dark cloud over my head. Every time I thought of something I needed to do, I would think of what I hadn't finished and feel guilty. It was a tremendous release when I did finally finish the project. I felt like I could breathe freely again. I could face the world. I could face my husband. I can now freely face new challenges. We need to finish what we start. Unfinished tasks waste our time and drain our mental peace. 'Even the woodpecker owes his success to the fact that he uses his head and keeps pecking away until he finishes the job he starts.'

An important habit that will keep us from wasting time is to have a place for everything and to put things back in their place when we finish using them. It wastes our time to make a big mess and then have to go back and clean it up. It's much easier and more

WHERE WILL I FIND THE TIME?

economical to clean up as we go along. McDonald's, the big hamburger restaurant chain, have the principle C.A.Y.G.—Clean As You Go—at the centre of their work. Now, some cooks may disagree about this. They would say 'When you cook you just make a big mess, and when you've finished you clean it up.' Well, I have to disagree. I've tried it both ways and I've also observed those who leave the mess until the end. I've concluded that you get more done more quickly and more efficiently if you clean as you go. The same applies to all areas of our lives. In our home, in our office, or wherever, have a place for everything and put everything back in its place. And train others in your family to do it too.

Another time-waster is 'busy work'—all those little things that come across our path. Keeping busy on trivia can give us a false sense of accomplishment. It's one of the greatest distractions the Enemy brings to us. We're busy, but only on the small things, the little details, that aren't so important. They keep us, in fact, from doing the really important things that God has for us. It's not how much we are doing that is important, but how much we get done of what God has called us to do. We can lose a lot of time on things that don't really count for God.

We can lose even more valuable time by getting involved in things that aren't really our business. We overhear a conversation and get drawn in. A friend shares what he or she is involved in, and instead of just offering advice, we step in.

Fear is yet another time bandit. Fear of failure, fear of making mistakes, fear of stepping out of the Lord's will, fear of making the wrong decision—all these can rob us of time to do what God has for us. Fear can waste our time as we sit around concentrating on the fear rather than moving ahead in faith on what God has given us to do. General George S. Patton said, 'There is a time to take counsel of your fears, and there is a time to never listen to any fear.' I believe we need to respond in a godly way to fear. Obviously, God wants us to work through it and come into a place of feeling secure in him. If we are loved by God and he is for us, then we need to remind ourselves—who can be against us? Even if we do make mistakes, God is right there to help us. In his wonderful creativity he can take our mistakes, turn them round, and bring good out of them. God wants us to accept the challenges and goals that he's given us. He doesn't want us to allow fear to drain away our time and prevent us from achieving those goals.

There are many more time bandits:

▷ procrastination: putting off what we have to do.

▷ meetings: especially those that are poorly planned and prepared for.

▷ paper work.

▷ unexpected guests.

▷ poor communication: not saying things clearly or to the right person.

▷ telephone calls.

▷ television.

The list could go on. We've looked at enough here to get the idea. We can each look at our own situations and spot the specific time bandits we face. For each time-waster we find, we need to try and find a solution as well.

Time for me

Once we've eliminated some of the 'trivial pursuits' that waste our time, we'll probably begin to see ways to plan in time for ourselves. We need to 'pencil' ourselves in—it's all part of scheduling. We need to allocate regular, uninterrupted time for things that we enjoy and that please us. Are other members of the family a problem? Remember, doors close as well as open. Most things can wait for a little while.

One of the first things we should do in making time for ourselves is to make sure we're getting adequate sleep and rest. A friend recently told me that she had to rearrange her schedule and 'work' towards resting. Many of us are like that. We feel guilty if we take a nap and condemned if we sit down to rest. But God rested. He found time to do it all—and do it well. And he knew rest was an important part of this. Jesus said, 'Come to me, all you who are weary and burdened, and I will give you rest' (Matthew 11:28).

One guideline for finding the balance between work and rest is to use the division of our day into thirds that we looked at in chapter 1. Use two-thirds of the day for work and one third for relaxation, family, etc. Whatever system we use or way we go about it, we must be sure to get the rest we need so we can function at our full capacity. God longs and desires for us to reach the full potential for which he's created us. 'He who knows us best, loves us most.' He wants to develop our gifts and talents. One of the biggest hindrances to this is our lack of self-acceptance, our insecurity, and our low self-esteem. In fact, many studies show these to be the number-one cause of depression and suicide —both of which are increasing at frightening rates for young and old, male and female. When we love ourselves, it's easier to love others and easier for them to love us.

There are some basic things we can do in dealing with a low self-image. We need, first of all, to be careful that we don't compare ourselves to one another. 2 Corinthians 10:12 tells us we are 'without understanding' or 'fools' when we do this. Our only measuring stick should be the Holy Spirit. We should let him set the standard for us.

We must also be careful that we do not accept defeat or failure in our lives. If we make mistakes, we must pick up the pieces and begin again. We must not dwell on the past. The God of the present doesn't hold past mistakes against us. History is full of examples of children who, according to their parents, peers or teachers, were total failures; but history has proved them wrong.

▷ Einstein was four years old before he could speak and seven before he learned to read.

▷ Beethoven's music teacher said of him, 'As a composer, he is hopeless.'

▷ A newspaper editor fired Walt Disney because Disney didn't have any good ideas.

▷ Werner von Braun failed algebra in his teens.

▷ Winston Churchill failed his exams even earlier.

They all made it in spite of difficult beginnings and discouragement from others.

We need to take positive steps to grow out of our insecurity. We need to work harder to be what we ought to be rather than hiding what we are. We must try to understand our insecurities and then ask the Lord's help in growing out of them. If we don't learn to accept ourselves, we will be falling into condemnation constantly.

87

We need to look in the mirror and thank God for the way he's made us. We need to be grateful, truly grateful, for who we are. The Bible says we must 'love our neighbour as ourselves'. If we do not love ourselves, we cannot fully love others. We must come to the place where we can say, with David, 'I will praise thee, for I am fearfully and wonderfully made.' We need to accept ourselves as we are. We can give God free rein to change areas that have been warped, and we can change some areas ourselves. We should not dwell on all the 'ifs': 'If I were taller;' 'If I had a different nose;' 'If I were rich.' That's a tragic way to live, and we will never be happy until we come to the place of accepting ourselves as God created us.

Looking good

In taking time for ourselves, another area we need to give attention to is the physical. Our body is a temple. Are we taking care of that temple? If we're in good condition physically, then we can use our time more effectively.

A few years ago, I realized my temple was badly in need of repairs and maintenance. I had gained unwanted weight with each of my two pregnancies. For a long time I had wanted to lose this weight. The problem was that every time I tried, I became ill. One day I was walking up the stairs to our fifth-floor apartment. I was carrying a heavy bag of groceries. Suddenly the thought came to me that I would always have to carry the groceries up, but if I weighed less it would certainly be a lot easier. I determined to find a healthy way to lose the weight I didn't want or need. I realized I wasn't getting any younger and it was harder to lose weight as the years went by. I began to pray and ask the Lord for a healthy weight-loss plan.

He gave me one and the end result was that I lost forty pounds in the next six months. I looked better, I felt better about myself, and I now knew that my temple was in good condition.

Once I'd lost all that weight, I could wear clothes that I'd always wanted to wear and couldn't. I could really be *me!* Each of us are like different flowers in the Lord's garden—all beautiful, but all different. No two are alike, just as no two snowflakes are alike. Suddenly I could be the flower I'd always wanted to be, the one God had created me to be. I began to phase out clothes in my wardrobe and take steps of faith in buying new ones. I was able to express myself in my style of dressing. My personal taste in a number of areas was one of the things I was able to work on in taking time for myself. As I did this my self-esteem grew as well.

Another area where we need to take time for life—for ourselves—is in the area of our gifts, talents and hobbies. God has deposited things in our lives, but some of them need to be developed. We need to take time for that. I've always wanted to draw and paint, but I'm not very good at it. Recently I talked to a friend who has had the same desire. She took some classes a couple of years ago and is now painting beautiful watercolours—and she didn't begin until she was over forty. I've been encouraged by that; there's still hope for me. I'm determined to find time for classes myself in the future. There are seeds planted in our lives that haven't had the opportunity to grow and develop because we haven't taken time to water them. We *must* find time to do that if we are going to be the individuals God wants us to be, if the gifts he has placed in our lives are going to be used to the fullest.

We work better and are more pleasant when we feel good about ourselves. This begins on the inside and then goes on to find outward expression. It's all part of 'looking good'. God is reflected through us both spiritually and physically. We serve a God of beauty and design. He wants to be seen in our lives in every way. We need to take time for some of these practical areas of our lives. It's not a waste of time to do so, but using our time in a balanced way. In the midst of finding time for all the various areas of our lives we must make sure we're making time to develop into the individuals God wants us to be.

When we are secure in who God made us to be, we can then fulfil his calling for our lives more fully. Our work can be lifted up as a sacrifice of service, rather than being proof of worthiness. Time for work will then be in balance in our lives.

7
A Time for Work

'A time to plant and a time to uproot' (Ecclesiastes 3:2)

Work! It's always there. We never seem to get it all done. It's part of life. If we don't give proper attention to the work God has for us, we're lazy and irresponsible. We must give the needed time and attention to what God has called us to do—be that a secular job or involvement in Christian ministry. One minute spent in planning saves three or four minutes in doing. We should never be too busy to stop and plan. There are practical ways for getting our work done in the time that we have. Some are very simple; others may call for rearranging our lifestyle.

We must, first of all, learn to say no. For many of us it is one of the hardest things we may ever have to do, and for some of us it will be the highest hurdle we face along the obstacle course of learning to organize our time. Unless we weigh the demands on our day carefully, we're bound to be left with too little time to meet our obligations. We must turn down things that are least important to us and schedule the things that really count.

When a demand is made on our time, we must evaluate it in terms of the goals and priorities we have set.

Delegating

A lot of this has to do with learning to delegate. None of us can do everything. You may think that delegation has only to do with working in an office or business. But it is relevant in almost every area of our life—home, family, church, neighbourhood. If you haven't learned to delegate, you are missing one of the keys God has for you in learning to use and manage your time properly. You can't do it all, and who wants to? When you try to, you usually end up feeling overwhelmed, resentful, and taken for granted. We need to become 'managers'—even in the home. Household managers. One of the key things managers know how to do is to delegate responsibility.

An important point in learning to delegate is to train first. We need to work with those around us. We need to train them, develop their gifts, and give them opportunities to learn and grow. If we don't do this, the time will come when we need to rely on them and they won't be ready.

When we delegate, we must give clear direction—what's to be done, how, when and where. Clarity in the beginning helps to avoid tension and frustration later. We often assume people know something or understand a situation when they don't. It's better to assume they don't and say it again.

We must look around us prayerfully and ask the Lord to show us the people he may be wanting us to work with more closely by sharing responsibility. Perhaps our children, a friend, a neighbour or a co-worker. Whom are we to train? To whom are we to give responsibility? Delegating and developing go hand in hand. We need to help people develop in their gifts and abilities. Then the opportunities will come to begin delegating things to them.

If you find it hard to let go of your work and to delegate, don't give up. Delegation is a skill you *can* learn. I found it hard to learn this skill because I am organized and detailed. I like things to be just right, and I hated giving jobs to others because I knew they wouldn't do them the way I wanted them to. It was very hard to let go of my responsibility. God very lovingly rebuked me. He let me know that if I tried to keep doing everything myself, I would not be able to grow into all that he had for me. He clearly asked me, 'Do you want to stay right where you are and just do what you are doing now, at the level of responsibility you have now, for the rest of your life? Or do you want to grow into some of the challenges that I have for you? If you want to grow, you must learn to let go, to delegate.'

We must learn to lean on others and stop trying to do it all ourselves. We must recognize that we are not self-sufficient and we need help. In fact we may even have to give up responsibilities that we really enjoy. Pride may hinder us from delegating as well. We may be more concerned with what people will think of us than with actually seeing the job finished.

Recently I went through an emotional struggle in turning over two very enjoyable responsibilities to other people. I had come to the place where I just couldn't keep doing them. There was so much more that God had given me to do. Something had to go, and it was selfish of me to hang on. These two particular things were a creative outlet for me. They were a job, but they were also creative and fun. I loved doing them. I argued with the Lord for several weeks before I obeyed what he had spoken to me to do. Now it's a real joy to stand back and watch the Lord developing these other people. Seeing other people in action has been almost as fulfilling to me as doing the job myself! I can now see that the Lord had other things that he wanted me to do, and that he also wanted to do something new, wonderful and fresh in these other people. I learned the secret of the joy of delegating. As we do it, the Lord is able to use us in leading others into new areas of fulfilment and responsibility. The umbilical cord has to be cut, so to speak. If we don't cut it, death will result—our death, because we can't cope with all that is before us.

Once we've decided to delegate, we need to decide on the job that needs to be done. What are the objectives of that job? What are the minimum standards for getting it done? What are the required results? Then we need prayerfully to get someone else to do it instead of ourselves. It's important to remember here that we can't presume on other people in delegation. We can't just hand out jobs to those around us. We must ask them sometimes to pray about it as well. When they do that, they have a sense of responsibility about the job. They need that because they are going to be the ones doing it. All this, as I've said, must be covered in prayer asking the Lord's help in working it out.

As you look at your schedule, your goals and your time budget, evaluate each new demand that comes into your life. See if it is going to work into your budget. Perhaps it needs to go to someone else—or something already in your budget needs to be turned over to someone to make room for this new item. Ask the Lord what can be done by others, and then learn the principle of delegation. It is a key in being able to do more for the Lord. If we don't learn to delegate, we cannot take on more in our homes, jobs or ministries.

And mums, don't by any means feel all this is not for you. You're not left out in this whole area. Does your home have 'kid power'? Use it! Learn to delegate to them too, and to your husband at times. Mobilize the troops in your home so you can do all the Lord has for you.

Personal energy level

I have a little plaque on a shelf in my living room that says, 'Everything I didn't do yesterday plus all I haven't done today plus all I won't do tomorrow—completely exhausts me!' Ever feel like that? It's important in looking at this whole area of time for work to examine our personal energy level. We need to plan our tasks according to our biological clocks. We must try to do the difficult tasks when we have most energy. We must plan in the different types of work we need to do at the time of day when we can do each one best. But we often go about it in just the opposite manner.

Look at your day and your lifestyle. When do you have most energy? Is it in the morning or evening? Some of us are night people. We get our best work done between 9 p.m. and 2 a.m. Find out when your energy level is highest and try to tackle the hard things you have to do then. Do the things you don't like doing then, too. You'll be able to give yourself to the fullest and get them done more easily and quickly.

I find my best time is at the beginning of the day when I am fresh (or hopefully I am fresh if I have had a fair amount of sleep the night before!) and before the interruptions of the day begin. I often get up an hour or so before the rest of the household—before the phone and doorbell start ringing, before Floyd and my children need me. I get up and do some of my hardest tasks before family life begins. To balance that, I sometimes take a half-hour nap in the afternoon. We must look at how God has made each of us. We don't all fit into a little box called 'time management' and do things exactly alike. We must look at our individual physical make-up—how God created us to be—and find the time of day when our energy level is at its highest. That's the time to do our hardest jobs.

It's good to look at our week in much the same way. At the beginning of the week, when we look over the things God has for us in the days ahead, we need to pinpoint the most difficult things in that week. Again, we may find it best to tackle those things at the beginning of the week when we are still fresh. Obviously, there are times when we have no control over when things must be done—they have to be done at a certain time. But more often than not we can control them. If possible, then, we can do those difficult tasks at a time in the week when we know we can give ourselves to them most fully.

Juggling

Juggling is a fairly accurate description of how we must manage to find the time for all our work. We suspend one job, catch another, and toss yet a third. One manual on learning how to juggle says that timing, concentration and co-ordination are essential. It looks so simple, but it's more than a little twist of the wrist. Let's look at these three vital aspects.

Timing is equally distributing our expectations and energy. Concentration is where organizing and planning come in. Co-ordination is making use of all the help we can get (delegating).

Our individual work situations require personalized plans. No two plans are alike. We should not feel intimidated if we go about accomplishing the work we have to do in a way that is different from everyone else. The important thing is to get the job done. When there is a lot to do, what do we do first? Which job gets immediate attention? Which voice gets heard? To break it down to its simplest terms we do one thing and then the next. As we come to each job, we need to look afresh at our goals and priorities, then do what needs to be done most in accordance with them in the amount of time we have to work with. If we only have an hour, what can we accomplish in that amount of time? What is the most important thing to give our attention to?

This morning I had planned to work on this chapter. My husband was getting ready to leave on a trip. He was trying to finish a writing project before he left. He needed my help unexpectedly to do that. He also needed my help in packing. I stopped working on my writing, helped him finish his, and got his suitcase packed. He's now on an aircraft somewhere and I'm back at the typewriter. That's juggling! We all have to do it at times.

We must also adjust our expectations for our work from time to time. I like everything to be perfect down to the finest detail, but most people don't care about all the fine details. There are times when I must let some of the details go in order to get a job done—for example, when we have guests over for dinner. I love to cook a big meal and set a beautiful table. There are times, though, when I have had to serve a very simple meal buffet style in order that the occasion actually take place! Fellowship and friendship were more important than a fancy table and an elegant meal. I had to adjust my expectations.

Every once in a while 'one of those days' will come along. They're inevitable. They happen to the most efficient of us as well as to the least. The purpose and blessing of being organized is that we don't have our disorganization to cope with as well as all the unexpected things that come along. So we have a little less 'juggling'!

Routine

Routine is not the answer to every schedule problem, but it can help to control a schedule that must also be flexible. Routine does not make you lose spontaneity, but allows you more time to do what you want. Assume your routine will be disrupted. Make a contingency plan. One wife I read about said she had plan A, B, C and D. It wasn't usually until mid-morning that she knew which plan it would be for the day.

Practical helps

We should tackle a big job in stages. This is sometimes called the 'salami' method of saving time and getting the work done. Look at the task in hand as a whole salami from which we can slice off a little bit each day. Where we would usually allocate one time during the day when we need to clean our desk, instead we can go through one drawer at a time. The job gets done more quickly, we are less apt to panic and feel overwhelmed, and we're less likely to put it off because it is too big. We can break big jobs down into realistic, workable parts.

We should take advantage of technology to help us in getting our work done. Technology may be daunting at times, but it can certainly make life easier. A microwave oven can help get us out of the kitchen in record time. A slow-cooker can cook dinner while we're away for the day. The phone can help keep a friendship growing when there's no time to visit—and (as we will see later) we can do other things at the same time. A computer can help in countless ways (especially in writing a book). I must confess that I have been intimidated by computers. They've seemed so complicated to me. I've put off learning to use one for ages, but Floyd insisted that I learn for working on this book. It was a huge challenge to me—a big mountain I didn't want to climb. Much to my surprise, it wasn't nearly as difficult as I had anticipated. I'm still learning, but the mountain isn't as high as I thought. We need to overcome our hesitations about technology and invest in tools that can help us use our time more wisely.

We need to practise doing two or three things at once. The 'juggling' act again. We can buy a shoulder attachment for our telephone that frees both hands. As we talk, we can do a number of things at once. For example, polish our nails and do leg exercises—all while we chat with a friend. We can clean out a drawer as we talk, sort mail, fold the laundry, iron clothes, wash dishes, chop vegetables, do the mending—the list is endless. We can write a list or letter while we wait in the car or travel on public transport. We can read a magazine while exercising on a stationary bike (one of my favourites!). We can read a book while waiting in the bank or department store—or waiting for someone to arrive at the airport or station. Many work activities can be doubled up with other things when we think creatively about using our time. This is part of finding 'lost' time. It's there, and we can put it to good use. We should also think of ways to consolidate. We can plan errands as efficiently as if our job were to schedule deliveries. It saves time and steps.

We must live in the present. We should be careful that we don't dwell on past mistakes or give in to anxiety about the future. Not only does this waste our valuable work time, but it also promotes joylessness and diminishes our efficienty. 'We can't change the past, but we ruin a perfectly good present by worrying about the future.'

We need to eliminate long, aimless phone conversations from our lives. A timer helps. Set it for five minutes—you'll be amazed at how much can get said in five minutes, at how much phone bills decrease, and at how much more time you have for work.

In looking at work, a key rule is to simplify, simplify, simplify. Make it as easy for yourself as you can. If it's easy to get done then it will get done, otherwise there's a good chance it won't. Arrange supplies you need so that they're handy. Don't strive for perfection. Combine unpleasant tasks (ironing) with something enjoyable (nice music). Each time we simplify we diminish stress and help to get the job done.

Women

In an address to 5,000 women, the present Prime Minister, Margaret Thatcher, said 'If you want something said, ask a man. If you want something done, ask a woman.' Men often don't appreciate how much women do. A lot is taken for granted simply because we usually do it. 'Division of labour is when your husband cleans the glove compartment and you clean the house.' However, most of us can't be Superwoman! Many of us have what one psychologist calls Type E behaviour—Everything to Everybody. Enough is Enough! We need to break out of the Superwoman syndrome.

A big part of many women's work is housework. Housework is family work—wife, husband, children. 'Most men can't find in their own kitchens what most women can find in a stranger's kitchen.' In the typical family what makes life comfortable for the man and the children is what makes life hard for the woman—

the housework. Studies show that today's housewife spends the same time or longer at housework as women did fifty years ago, in spite of all our modern helps. There's more to be done, more space to be taken care of, and jobs are done more often and more thoroughly. Most men are not aware of this fact. They tend to think they've done their bit by buying a washing machine, tumble dryer or microwave for the home in order to help the wife save time and energy. These certainly help, but nothing can replace the helping hands that are needed to get all the jobs done.

A whole book could be written (and many have been) on hints that help in getting the work done in the home. Let's look at just a few basic ones here that will help to simplify, organize and keep things running smoothly.

▷ Find a place for everything (and keep everything in its place).

    (a) If you haven't read it in twelve months—toss it!

    (b) If you haven't worn it in two years—give it away!

    (c) If you haven't used it in three years—discard it!

    (d) Be ruthless! Force yourself to get over the 'maybe I'll use it someday' syndrome.

▷ Keep drawers and cupboards clean as you go so you won't have to spend a day or two doing all of them at once.

▷ Mend clothing or sew on buttons as you iron. Keep needles and thread handy near the ironing board.

▷ Get a head start on your family. Organize and plan ahead of time so things run smoothly when the time comes.

▷ Set up a system of household information: a filing cabinet, folders or a loose-leaf binder. Keep shopping lists, phone numbers, timetables, sample menus, etc. available for everyone. It keeps others from helping out if Mum is the only one with the information.

▷ A central notice-board is vital so that everyone knows where to look for important messages.

▷ Keep cleaning supplies handy and accessible so everyone can use them.

There is a time for work and that work will go better when we put effort into planning and organizing so that we can get more done. 'What counts is not the number of hours we put in, but how much we put into those hours.' Still, we will probably never get it all done. Take heart—we're in good company. Dr Bob Pierce once encouraged me with these wise words: 'Don't fail to do something just because you can't do everything.'

In planning time for work, we must be careful to balance it with fun.

8

A Time for Fun

'A time to weep and a time to laugh, a time to mourn and a time to dance' (Ecclesiastes 3:4).

'Slow down or you'll miss the scenery.' In the midst of organizing, planning, being efficient, and using our time well we must make sure that we stay balanced. We can be in such a hurry to 'do' for God that we miss the simple pleasures in life. We can be in such a hurry in accomplishing things, that we don't enjoy the world around us. We must *slow down*, relax and have fun.

All our time belongs to God. As I've said before, time is a gift for us to use. We're stewards of it, and accountable for our use of it. We're to glorify God in what we do with our time. We're to use it well and 'redeem' it, not waste it. But we must be balanced. In our time budget we should invest our time, not just spend it. One of the best investments we can make is to relax and do enjoyable things. Contrary to what we often think, busyness is not related to godliness.

Amy Carmichael gives what I think is a clear definition of relaxation and recreation: 'Re-equipment for work with no leakage of spiritual power.' We must take time for fun and relaxation if we're to be at our best for God. We often don't relax or enjoy today because we're so busy worrying about tomorrow. In fact, before we can relax we must turn off our 'worry switch'. I've heard it said that 'worry is interest paid on trouble before it is due'. We can drain our energy and resources worrying about things that may never even happen. The Bible tells us we're not to be anxious—it wastes time and it won't really help anything. Worrying about what is not done will never get it done. We must give our worries and cares to the Lord so we are free to relax.

Some of us need to experience the 'joy' of doing nothing for a full five minutes. For many of us, it would be almost impossible. We need to 'do' nothing . . . let our minds roam . . . let God bring creative, inspirational thoughts to us . . . let him minister to us in the stillness. I read of a well-known novelist who worked for years in a humdrum, routine, undemanding job. He used that time to its fullest advantage by letting his mind develop plots for his books.

We should explore ways to do a little of what pleases us, the things we enjoy, every day. We've already looked at taking time for ourselves, but it bears repeating here in the context of relaxation and fun. We need to block out time in our schedule for ourselves. No doubt we've all heard the saying that 'all work and no play makes Jack a dull boy'. It also makes him an unbalanced boy. We'll never develop our full potential, our full personality, if we don't take time for fun. We take, or make, time for everything else in our lives. We must be careful not to miss this area.

Have you ever been enjoying a film, reading a book, watching television, listening to music, walking through a museum, and suddenly found yourself feeling guilty? Why is that? Often it's because we remember all the things we have to do. We feel guilty taking time for fun, for pleasure. It is not a sin to have fun! If we carry this guilt around with us we will miss the enjoyment and refreshment of fun and relaxation. God is a God of fun. I think he believes in having an enjoyable time. He blessed the wedding feast at Cana. He didn't condemn them for having a happy celebration.

I also think God has a sense of humour (he must have to put up with some of the things we do!). He probably likes a good joke. After all, he created laughter. It is not an accident that it takes less muscles to smile (thirteen) than it does to frown (sixty-four). Smiling has a positive physical effect on us. 'The world looks brighter from behind a smile.' It's good for us. Did you know that your body will not let you laugh and develop an ulcer at the same time? Laughter has tremendous healing power. It's medicine for the soul. Take time for laughter.

Maybe you feel too pushed to stop and have fun, too under pressure to finish a job or meet a deadline. Do it anyway. If you're a 'high achiever' or 'workaholic', you probably tend to overschedule both your work and your personal life. Relaxation? It may have never occurred to you. In fact, you may not even know what relaxing means. You may even have lost touch with the whole idea of taking care of yourself. You will never be able to enjoy the things you're doing, the people you're with, or the job you're involved in if you can't relax. People who are relaxed work better and have better health. Learning to relax makes sense.

Regular fun and relaxation are as important, if not more so, than the amount of time we have for them. A few minutes or an hour will often do more good for us than several days of relaxation time that we've been waiting for for weeks.

It's also important to relax by doing things we like to

do. Often we follow someone else's prescription for fun, but find it's not enjoyable to us. We need to understand what is relaxing and fun for us and do that. If you're not sure, experiment and find things that are fun for you.

Learn to relax

There are some simple, basic things we can do to relax— things that will even help relieve tension and refresh us.

(1) Pause

Pausing can change our situation and frame of mind, erasing where we are and preparing us to begin again. Without pausing, our attention stays focused on the situation or problem we're in. We're 'locked' into the tension and pressure of the moment. Pausing can help us break out of it.

(2) Breathe

When I'm under pressure I get tense in my shoulders. My daughter often rubs them for me to help me relax. She tells me, 'Take a deep breath now and relax.'

Taking a deep breath helps break tension. There are four phases to this kind of breathing. Inhale, pause, exhale, pause. When we do this several times we can feel the tensions melting away. Breathing deeply will also help clear the 'cobwebs' out of our brains so that we can think more clearly as we resume our work.

(3) Move

When you're tensed up from stress, get up and walk around for a few minutes. Movement of any kind, actually, helps to reduce tension. Yawning, stretching, tapping your foot (ever wondered why some people do that a lot?), walking—all help to get rid of tension.

(4) *Take a break*

We think we don't have time to stop, but it's the best thing we can do. Are your teeth clenched? Neck tight? Shoulders bunched up? Biting your fingernails? Staring off into nowhere? Chewing the inside of your mouth? All these are signs of tension. They're showing us that we need to have a break. Focus on relaxing these tension points. You'll feel better immediately and be in better shape to resume the task in hand.

I once saw a list someone had made of what were called 'breathers for a busy day'. They were practical suggestions for little breaks.

Take Two (minutes!):

▷ potter with a plant . . . like a two-minute trip to the country.

▷ peel an orange . . . delicious aroma and refreshing taste.

▷ write a quick postcard . . . you'll be pleased to have done it and a friend will love hearing from you.

▷ have a quick dip . . . splash cold water on your face . . . nice and refreshing on your wrists too.

▷ put your feet up.

▷ read a few jokes . . . and don't be too self-conscious to laugh.

▷ yell . . . great tension and frustration reliever . . . just choose carefully where you do it!

Take Five:

▷ Turn on some music . . . let your body unwind as you move to the music.

▷ Clear up the clutter . . . tidy up your workspace. You'll feel better about beginning again.

▷ Phone a friend to say a quick hello. Reaching out to someone can be refreshing.

▷ Relive a happy experience. The joy of it will be fresh all over again.

▷ Flip through a cookery book, catalogue or dictionary. One of my father's favourite ways to relax was to read the encyclopedia!

Take Ten:

▷ Take a quick walk.

▷ Knit a few rows of something you're making.

▷ Watch television for a while.

▷ Read a page in a devotional book.

A few minutes may not seem like much of a break, but you'll be surprised at the benefit it can bring. Change is one of the best refreshments there is. When you do something different for a few minutes, it's amazing how much better you'll feel.

Time use

We need to be on guard that we don't devote precious 'free time' to everyday work. Perhaps we've been in need of some relaxation time, some time just to have fun. God opens up the opportunity and gives it to us, but we use it to 'catch up' on housework, etc. It's like a slap in the face. We've been given a special gift, and we don't receive it.

I often hear people say, 'I just don't have enough time. There's not enough time to relax and have fun.'

Jean de la Bruyère said, 'Those who make the worst use of their time are the first to complain of its shortness.' We must plan our time, use it well, and make sure there's a place for fun.

When we do make time for fun, we often try to pack in too much. One researcher I read said that people often feel they're missing out on fun. When they get time for it they try to make up for it with a schedule that leaves them physically wiped out instead of being refreshed. They try to cram too much activity into too short a time.

We often miss it on timing too. When the daily grind is starting to wear us down, that's when we need to take a break—be it for a few minutes or a few days. Many of us just put it off. We need to stop putting off pleasure. Spontaneity is a key word. Our schedule and our planning is a blessing and help, but we are not to become slaves to it. We must be in control and able to break out of it when we need to. Everyone needs relaxation, fun, time away. This cannot be emphasized enough. It's crucial to our well-being, vital for our physical and emotional health.

I encourage you to have a 'fun-pot'. A jar, piggy bank, envelope or whatever where you can save for these fun times. It doesn't need to be a lot, but just a little extra set aside for doing something different and enjoyable in order to relax.

Procrastination

I can almost hear some of you reacting as you're reading all this. 'This just isn't me.' 'I've got too much to do for God for all this frivolous fun stuff.' Maybe you're a 'pleasure shirker'. People can stall at having a good time as much as they can put off unpleasant tasks. We need to work out what's getting in the way:

▷ Is it the guilt feeling I mentioned earlier? 'I haven't worked hard enough to deserve a break.'

▷ Or maybe it's the 'I don't want to make a fool of myself' excuse. Someone suggests an idea for relaxation, but you're afraid you'll look foolish. 'I'll embarrass myself playing tennis.' 'No one will like my art.' 'I'd look stupid out jogging at my age.'

▷ Perhaps you're caught in the 'indecision dilemma'. You don't know what to do to relax—and you lose the time for it while you're trying to decide what to do.

▷ We worry about what others will think. 'I know people will think I've lost out with God if I take that time off.' Maybe we should be more concerned about what God will think if we don't.

The list of procrastinations is endless. A procrastinator is one who won't take *now* for an answer. We can't afford to postpone having fun. We need it, right now. Whatever our excuse, we must face it honestly, deal with it appropriately, and begin to enjoy the rest God wants us to have.

Creativity

There's another reason why taking time to relax is important. Relaxing time is anything that helps us break out of our routine in order to allow other, hidden parts of ourselves to come alive. Michael Foster says, 'Leisure is the mother of discovery.' All of us have untapped resources that are just waiting to be developed. That will never happen if we don't provide the time for creativity to spring to the surface and grow. Today's dreams become tomorrow's realities. Everything that has ever been achieved started first as an unseen spark in someone's creative imagination. The sparks seem to flow more easily when we make a relaxed environment for them to grow in.

I'm not talking about creating some masterpiece. I'm simply pointing out the relaxation, the fun, the enjoyment and the therapy of giving ourselves the opportunity to be creative. 'Joy is the process of doing what we love, not the end result.' We serve a creative God, and he wants to find expression in our lives in creative ways.

We need to provide the time to 'unlock' all that God has put in us. A few years ago I began to understand that God had planted in me an ability for decorating— for being able to create warm, pleasant surroundings that reflected his character. My love for 'details' was even part of that creative expression. It was all part of who God had made me to be and what he had deposited in my life. I could 'create' with him.

One Nobel prize winner has said, 'Discovery consists of seeing what everybody has seen and thinking what nobody has thought.' As we take time to relax, those thoughts can flow.

There's a time for 'everything under the sun', including having fun. Maybe this is a 'skill' that some of us still need to learn. There's no better time to start learning than now. As we develop this skill, perhaps it will bring balance into our lives so that we don't need time for healing.

9
A Time for Healing

'A time to kill and a time to heal, a time to tear down and a time to build' (Ecclesiastes 3:3).

Trying to cope with the demands of life—planning, organizing and scheduling them—puts us in what I call the 'pressure cooker' of life. The intensity of it all can harm us. The doing, serving and giving tires us out. We feel stretched in fifty different directions—all at once. The wear and tear of life begins to take its toll. We may develop 'hurry sickness' or the 'achiever's disease'. 'Burn-out' has become a very common modern-day disease of the overcommitted. It is brought on as a result of chronic stress in our lives. Stress is known as the 'silent killer'. It's the consequence of overuse of our body, mind and emotions. Burn-out, in fact, slows us down before stressful destruction. Too much stress can ruin our health and even shorten our life. We may find ourselves in the unexpected place of needing healing.

No one is immune from stress and pressure—new Christians, old Christians, leaders, ministers—we all face it. If we find ourselves 'wiped out', it doesn't mean we're abnormal, weak or a failure as a Christian.

What it does mean is that we need to take better control over our time and schedule. It is not God's plan for us to feel frantic. If we're frantic, we've lost control. We need to look at the things in our life or the hours in our day over which we have no control.

We want our capacity increased, not our load decreased. We don't want to do less for the Lord. Hudson Taylor in the book *Hudson Taylor's Spiritual Secret* is quoted as saying, 'It doesn't matter, really, how great the pressure is. It only matters where the pressure lies. See that it never comes between you and the Lord—then, the greater the pressure, the more it presses you to His breast.'

The Bible doesn't teach that we will be free of stress, but it does tell us how to deal with it. We're told to cast our burdens on the Lord. We're reminded that his power is made perfect in our weakness. We're encouraged that his grace is sufficient for our every need. Paul says a lot about stress. In 2 Corinthians 1:10 he says that he is grateful to God who has, will and will continue to deliver us. He learned that gratitude through suffering, great pressure and despair as he saw the power of God at work (verses 8-9). He speaks about being 'hard pressed on every side . . . perplexed . . . persecuted . . . struck down'. But it taught him about God's power. At the end he could say he was 'not crushed . . . not in despair . . . not abandoned . . . not destroyed' (2 Corinthians 4:8-9). He found God faithful to meet him as he faced immense stress, stress of the type that few of us will ever experience. For each one of us there is always time and energy for God's will in our lives—even when it's stressful.

Causes

Stress is dangerous when it is unduly prolonged.

Intensity is the key factor. In order to understand this modern-day illness, we need to know what causes it. There are many 'germs', but let's look here at a few of the common ones.

▷ Taking on too much responsibility, usually out of a sincere desire to serve God.

▷ Poor time management: not using the time we have well.

▷ An inability to work effectively with those around us.

▷ One-track mind: a lack of variety and diversion in our lives.

▷ Unrealistic expectations.

▷ Unfulfilled expectations, disappointments.

▷ A lack of affirmation and encouragement.

▷ Conflict at work or home.

▷ Fear: of what people think, death, loss of money, property or looks, failure, etc.

▷ Resentment: towards God or people around us.

▷ An inability to adjust to new people and new situations.

▷ An inability to relax.

▷ Wrong priorities.

▷ Criticism.

Refuelling

In order to resist the 'germs' that cause the 'illness', it is important to understand our individual 'threshold' and how to work with it. Our body gives us clues that say to us, 'Be careful! You're on dangerous territory.'

They are like little warning signals, flashing amber lights that say, 'Slow down—danger ahead.' Unfortunately, we often fail to heed them. Things like frequent headaches, fatigue, a low energy level, irritability, boredom, insomnia, forgetfulness, crying, feeling overwhelmed and feeling trapped are all 'symptoms' that something is wrong.

I've learned through the years that I have two little physical danger signs. I normally have a great memory, especially for details. When I'm pushing too hard, I forget all kinds of things. I also start to ache in my lower back. I've learned to pay attention to these signals—they're my body's way of telling me to be careful. Stress has been linked with almost every known human disease. The relationship between them is not always clear, but stress seems to aggravate any tendency towards disease. When we don't follow biblical, godly principles for our lives and work, we often suffer the consequences.

In understanding our threshold, we need to know our pressure points. What are our energy resources? What builds us up? For me, it's a quiet evening at home, a few extra hours of sleep, or being able to relax and read a book. We also need to know what drains our energy; what takes away those resources. A full, busy schedule, heavy counselling sessions, long days of housework, and having a lot of guests in our home leave me lacking in the resources I need to press on.

Our 'inner batteries' need to be recharged. When we know what depletes their power, we can learn to recognize when we're charged up and plan our busy times accordingly. As we begin to recognize the things that drain and wear us down, we can watch and be on guard not to push too far. We can get the needed refreshment before we've gone beyond our limits. We must be careful not to ignore the warning signals. If we do not 'come apart and rest a while', we may plain come apart! Psalm 103:14 tells us that 'he knows how we are formed, he remembers that we are dust'. Nothing is accomplished by being a martyr and burning ourselves out by working too hard. We need to learn our limitations and then work within them. We need to learn how to be 'refuelled'.

If you are a perfectionist, you may need to lower your standards a little—you can always improve. The first step in anything we do should always be small and manageable, something we can handle. If we begin by expecting perfection, we will never get there. I have had to learn this. I enjoy teaching. I love to study for and put together a teaching lesson. But I have a tendency to want my message to be perfect the first time I speak it out. I realize that this is unrealistic. I need to start with where I am right now. As I begin sharing on a topic, God will teach me and refine that area of my life. He will keep giving me new insights and thoughts, and new understanding of his ways and principles. I've learned that when I have the challenge of teaching before me, I must begin by doing the best that I can. But I also realize that my message is far from perfect. I've got a lot to learn. If I teach on the same subject ten years later, it will probably be much better.

We shouldn't be afraid of making mistakes. It's like a child learning to walk. Have you ever watched a baby learning to take his first steps? First of all he holds on to something and takes a step. Then he lets go and takes a step, falls, cries a little, then he crawls for a while. Pretty soon he plucks up courage again. He stands up and tries all over again. It is painful to watch him as he falls, tries again, falls, tries again, falls, tries again. Do you know that God gives us that same freedom of learning to walk in the things he has for us? Let yourself make mistakes—God gives you that freedom. Don't be afraid of them, but be willing to learn and grow with them.

In learning how to refuel ourselves, we need to learn to take short breaks (as mentioned in previous chapters) that can build us up. I've mentioned how I sometimes take a short nap in the afternoon to compensate for getting up so early in the morning. As I've done this, I've noticed the Lord developing something within me that hasn't been there before. I've always envied Floyd's ability to sleep anywhere, anytime. It seems to be a blessing from the Lord that enables him to cope with a schedule that includes a lot of travel, time changes, jet lag, etc. He can sit down and be asleep in five minutes.

I've never been able to do this. There have been times when we have had an hour or so to rest before a meeting or appointment. Floyd would lie down and be sound asleep in minutes; I'd be a bundle of tension, totally unable to relax.

I've often prayed and asked the Lord to do something that would help me to be refreshed in short amounts of time. Something wonderful has happened! There is no explanation except that God has answered my prayer. I can now lie down to rest, drop into a deep sleep in five minutes, and awake refreshed ten minutes later, feeling like a new person. I've never been able to do this before. I believe God has done something in my body chemistry to help refuel me and keep me built up in order to cope with the tasks he's put before me. He can do this kind of thing for each of us. He tells us in Matthew 11:28, 'Come to me, all you who are weary and burdened, and I will give you rest.' He loves to refresh us.

Maybe you're not a person that can take a short nap, but you can sit down and read for ten minutes. You're refreshed in this way by getting your mind off your activities. Maybe a ten-minute walk out in the fresh air does the trick. Whatever it is, do it. Find the things that refuel you. Even plan them into your daily schedule. We need to take advantage of these little things that keep us functioning at our best for the Lord.

We also need to look at what we're eating. There's a saying that we are what we eat, and there's a lot of truth in that. If we fill ourselves up with junk food, we're going to be working on junk in order to fulfil our responsibilities. We're not going to have much energy. We need to look at our diet carefully to see what we're putting into our temple of the Holy Spirit. God may want to speak to us about this.

If we have a very strenuous schedule, we particularly need protein input that will lift our energy level. We may need to take vitamins. A few years ago I used to catch every sickness that came along. Every cold, every virus, every flu bug that went around, I got it. I came to a point of being so frustrated with this that again I asked the Lord's help in changing this area of my physical make-up. One of the things the Lord specifically spoke to me about was taking vitamins. This may not be for everybody, but it was something I needed to do. Since that time my health has improved dramatically. I've even gone through winters now without getting *any* colds or flu. I don't think that is a coincidence or good luck. I believe God answered my prayer in showing me how to improve my health. We can take these specific things to the Lord. It's part of using our time effectively. We'll have more time to do what God has for us when we're in good health and functioning in full strength.

In an article 'Is There Life after Burn-out?' (*New Wine* magazine, February 1985) Bruce Longstreth said that there is no easy cure for burn-out, but any good prescription would include three things:

▷ Conviction: seeing that there is a problem and wanting to change.

▷ Confession: admitting to the Lord and those we're close to that we've made mistakes.

▷ Counsel: seeking advice and making the necessary changes.

Prevention

Of course, we can also protect ourselves from the 'illness' before we ever get it. My mother always told me, 'An ounce of prevention is worth a pound of cure.' We need to find ways of reducing stress in our lives—practical things we can do in our organizing and scheduling. We can also ask God to increase our 'pressure quotient'. God can work in our lives in such a way that our capacity to handle pressure grows. I've often prayed for this. The things I face in my life as a matter of course now would have probably put me in hospital with a nervous breakdown ten years ago. The Lord has helped me to grow in this area of my life, and he's shown me his ways for responding to the increased load.

I love living in Holland. There are so many things about this land and its culture that fascinate me. One of the things I've been particularly interested in is the lovely old windmills. One of my Dutch friends told me about some of the history behind these landmarks. When they were first put into use, people had some problems with them. Sometimes the wind would catch the sails and they would turn so quickly that they would catch alight and burn up. They had to work on safety precautions to prevent this happening. Before they could do this, many were destroyed. The difficulty was not in catching the wind but in controlling it.

We're a bit like those windmills. It's no problem to find lots to do. The problem is in maintaining a balance and keeping ourselves from being 'burned up' and destroyed. A few years ago I was asked to speak at a large gathering of Christian workers on the topic of burn-out. I wondered if they thought I'd had a lot of experience with it and was thus qualified to teach on the subject! Anyway, here are a few suggestions that I found helpful, which I think we can all benefit from:

▷ Learn to be flexible. Only the gospel is unchanging! Flexibility reduces the likelihood of frustration.

▷ Learn that you can't do it all. We should accept that and pace ourselves. We also need to humble ourselves and ask for help when we need it.

▷ Re-order your priorities. Make sure you're maintaining balance in all areas of your life.

▷ Establish realistic goals.

▷ Learn to accept things you cannot change.

▷ Don't face things before you have to. His grace is sufficient when the need is there, not before.

▷ Take good care of yourself physically. Diet, exercise, rest and recreation should all be part of this.

▷ Receive encouragement when it's given. Don't brush it off by saying, 'Oh it was the Lord.' Certainly the Lord helps us, but you've been involved. You need that affirmation.

▷ Include variety in your life and schedule.

▷ Slow down! God is never in a hurry.

▷ Plan adequate time for spiritual nourishment and growth.

▷ Maintain a sense of humour. You need to be able to laugh at yourself.

▷ Use your common sense. That's why God gave it to you!

▷ Work at maintaining a positive attitude. A negative one is draining.

▷ Learn from your mistakes. When something goes wrong, it's not the end of the world.

▷ Keep prayer and praise in your heart continually.

When we take good care of ourselves consciously and without apology, we have the best chance of serving God for a long time.

Positive stress

It's also important to be aware of what one person called 'the blessing of being tense'. Not all stress is negative. Stress is involved in the mundane aspects of daily life. Getting out of bed in the morning can be stressful! If we tried to eliminate all stress from our lives, we wouldn't be alive.

There are some stresses and tensions that we *cannot avoid*. Some stress is good. It activates the flow of adrenalin which increases energy production, raises blood pressure, and accelerates the flow of oxygen into the body. Stress can help us deal with everyday life and unexpected crises. It stimulates us to manage the problems of life and adapt to change. Without some amount of stress, we would not be able to get up every day and go about our work.

There are some stresses and tensions that we *can avoid*. We create a lot of stress for ourselves. We pack too much into our schedules. We overcommit ourselves. We push ourselves too long and too hard. We don't take time for all the things we've talked about in this book.

There are some stresses and tensions that we *should not avoid*. Anything worth doing will involve stress. If we're going to be faithful servants of the Lord Jesus, it will involve stress. If we're going to reach out to people in need, it will involve stress. If we're going to attempt to live in harmony with brothers and sisters in the body of Christ, stress will be involved in working out difficulties in our relationships. It would be a serious mistake to avoid stress at any cost—we would miss what God has for us in many areas, and we would miss much of the richness of life.

The last verse of a poem by Annie Johnson Flint has often helped me keep it all in perspective:

> One day at a time,
>   and the day is His day;
> He hath numbered its hours,
>   though they haste or delay.
> His grace is sufficient;
>   we walk not alone;
> As the day, so the strength
>   that He giveth His own.

Proverbs 11:1 says, 'The Lord abhors dishonest scales, but accurate weights are his delight.' Burn-out, 'hurry sickness' and 'achiever's disease' are all imbalance. God wants to show us how to put the scales right again. He wants to bring healing. He wants to refresh us, restore us and give us a new beginning. We need to take time for this healing work to take place and for the recovery process to be put into operation. There is, thankfully, a time for healing when we've become 'sick' from the cares of life. Remember, when the pressures are great, God is in control—and he's not nervous!

A Last Word

The purpose of learning to use our time well is to be all God wants us to be and to do all God wants us to do. We don't want to be like the person in this poem when we face our Creator one day.

He was going to be all that a mortal could be . . .
    tomorrow.
No one would be kinder, or braver than he . . .
    tomorrow.
A friend who was troubled and weary, he knew,
    who'd be glad of a lift and who needed it, too; on
    whom he would call and see what he could do . . .
    tomorrow.
Each morning he stacked up the letters he'd write . . .
    tomorrow.
And he thought of the folks he would fill with delight
    . . . tomorrow.
It was too bad, indeed, he was busy today, and
    hadn't a minute to stop on his way. 'More time I'll
    have to give others,' he'd say . . . tomorrow.
The greatest of workers this man would have been
    . . . tomorrow.

The world would have known him had he ever seen
    . . . tomorrow.
But the fact is, he died and he faded from view. And
    all that he left here when living was through, was a
    mountain of things he intended to do . . .
    tomorrow.

Author unknown

Further Reading

Emilie Barnes, *More Hours in My Day* (Eugene, OR, Harvest House, 1982).

Jo Berry, *Managing Your Life and Time* (Grand Rapids, MI, Zondervan, 1986).

Edward R. Dayton and Ted W. Engstrom *Strategy for Living* (Ventura, CA, Regal Books, 1976).

Edward R. Dayton, *Tools for Time Management* (Grand Rapids, MI, Zondervan, 1974).

Ted W. Engstrom and Alec R. MacKenzie, *Managing Your Time* (Grand Rapids, MI, Zondervan, 1974).

Ted W. Engstrom, *The Pursuit of Excellence* (Grand Rapids, MI, Zondervan, 1982).

Donna Goldfein, *Everywoman's Guide to Time Management* (Berkeley, CA, Celestial Arts, 1977).

Alan Lakein, *How to Get Control of Your Time and Your Life* (New York, Signet Books, 1973).

Gordon MacDonald, *Ordering Your Private World* Crowborough, East Sussex, Highland, 1985).

Anne Ortlund, *The Disciplines of a Beautiful Woman* (Waco, TX, Word Books, 1977).

Charlie W. Shedd, *Time for All Things* (Nashville, TN, Abingdon, 1962).

Bonnie Wheeler, *The Hurrier I Go* (Ventura, CA, Regal Books, 1985).

Rick Yohn, *Finding Time* (Waco, TX, Word Books, 1984).